No APOLOGY NEEDED

LEARNING TO FORGIVE AS GOD DOES

No APOLOGY NEEDED

NATHAN BYRD

WHITAKER
HOUSE

No Apology Needed
Learning to Forgive as God Does

Nathan R. Byrd
Jesus Makes the Difference Ministries, Inc.
P.O. Box 8102
Greenwich, CT 06836
www.JesusMakesTheDifference.com

ISBN: 978-1-64123-121-3
eBook ISBN: 978-1-64123-122-0
Printed in the United States of America
© 2019 by Nathan R. Byrd

Whitaker House
1030 Hunt Valley Circle
New Kensington, PA 15068
www.whitakerhouse.com

Library of Congress Cataloging-in-Publication Data (Pending)

1 2 3 4 5 6 7 8 9 10 11 ⨀ 26 25 24 23 22 21 20 19

CONTENTS

PART ONE:

REDISCOVERING JEWISH RHYTHMS OF FORGIVENESS

1

YOM KIPPUR AND THE POWER OF FORGIVENESS

There are certain moments in your life that feel like an earthquake. The initial tremor alone jolts you off your feet!

My "second call" to ministry began with one of those moments. On a frigid winter night in January 2002, Dr. Morgan, a Messianic Jew, walked into a black Baptist church. He nonchalantly looked around and did not seem fazed by the small attendance. Later, I invited him into my office and we began some introductory small talk.

I apologized for the low attendance due to the weather, saying I felt sorry he had made the trip in vain. Standing in my office, he had no way of knowing that I was in my last year of pastoring—period. After three years of grinding away as a senior pastor, I was ready to leave all the church drama behind. I was having trouble enrolling the congregation in my vision for a multi-ethnic, non-denominational church community. Thus, his response to my apology shocked me.

"What if I'm not here for them? What if I'm here for you?"

At that very moment, I realized I was about to have an encounter with destiny.

Dr. Morgan then explained the difference between a Christian who understands the Jewish roots of their faith and one who does not. Every point he made had a drastic effect on my overall theology and shaped my ideas about forgiveness.

After that evening, Dr. Morgan and I began to meet regularly. He showed me the Hebraic basis of our Christian faith and how to interpret Scripture in light of that perspective. For about two years, Dr. Morgan mentored me. It is due to his worldview that I describe my current ministry, The Worship Center, as a Judeo-Christian ministry.

About a decade after I met Dr. Morgan, while running The Worship Center, I felt called to fast for a week. To be honest, I didn't really know what I was doing. I just knew God wanted me to focus on Him. That week turned out to be life-changing in more ways than I could have imagined.

YOM KIPPUR IS ALL ABOUT FORGIVENESS FROM GOD AND RESTORATION.

I had four conversations about forgiveness and reconciliation during my week of fasting. By the time Saturday night rolled around, it dawned on me that the previous Wednesday was Yom Kippur, the holiest day of the Jewish year. I was preparing for my sermon for the following morning when this revelation hit me, so I switched topics and prepared a message about Yom Kippur. Even so, I lamented. Despite all my meetings with Dr. Morgan, I had once again missed an opportunity to celebrate Yom Kippur.

Yom Kippur is all about forgiveness—from God, for Israel. It's all about restoration. The matter of forgiveness and how it is introduced in the Scriptures should be a primary matter in our churches. Yom Kippur, in many ways, is about recognition—of our sins against God and others—and that recognition directly impacts how we practice our faith.

That Sunday in September 2012, I started teaching a four-part series on Yom Kippur and the concepts of forgiveness and unforgiveness. It was as much for me as it was for the congregation. Within the context of my study and teaching, God began to give me a revelation about forgiveness, and it was one I had never heard during my forty-plus years of salvation. What God revealed was revolutionary to me and to those at The Worship Center. Many of us were convicted and challenged on the spot to reevaluate our views of forgiveness.

As the clarity of the revelation began to formulate in my mind, the first thing I realized was that this particular issue has been the enemy's main tool in destroying the unity and community of the church. Once he is able to distort a relationship in this area—and he does it often and effectively—he can collapse the potential of any couple, family, church, society, or nation. This particular issue has catastrophic results whether you are Christian or not—and whether you are religious or not. If we are not conscious of forgiveness, we become low-hanging fruit for the enemy and he picks us off at will.

Many books have been written on the subject of forgiveness from various theological viewpoints and I do not write this book to replace or undermine any of them. Instead, I hope this book will complement them and the matter of forgiveness may take on even greater significance for the church and body of Christ. So as you embark on this journey to comprehend, appreciate, and apply forgiveness, may the Holy Spirit be available to you. I hope you will reap the full benefits of forgiveness in your life and walk in its power.

2

ROSH HASHANAH AND GOD'S REMINDER TO REPENT

The Jewish New Year begins with a holiday called Rosh Hashanah, which translates literally as "Head of the Year." In modern Judaism, it is a wonderful time of celebration highlighting the creation of Adam and Eve. Each year, the celebration is treated like an anniversary of God's creation of humanity and time itself. Rosh Hashanah celebrations highlight the special relationship between YHWH (Yahweh or God) and humanity, as opposed to any of His other created life forms. In humanity, God created a mirror of Himself and deposited it in a container called flesh. The image of God is the essence of the unique connection between YHWH and humanity. (See Genesis 1:27.)

The celebration of Rosh Hashanah also includes the recognition of humanity's dependence on God as Creator, Sustainer, and Judge of the earth. Rosh Hashanah is a reminder to begin the year by looking toward God with admiration and praise.

From Rosh Hashanah forward—with its emphasis on our dependence on God—the Jewish calendar emphasizes the need for a right relationship with God and thus forgiveness. Rosh Hashanah—called the Feast of Trumpets in the Bible—begins a season of repentance. (See Leviticus 23:23–25; compare Psalm 81.) As a celebration, Rosh Hashanah has the power to set the tone for our entire year.

Through celebrating Rosh Hashanah at The Worship Center, I have seen the difference it can make in people's lives. I believe every church can benefit from incorporating Rosh Hashanah into their calendar.

A REMINDER TO LOOK TO GOD

Rosh Hashanah reminds us that throughout the year, we should look to God for His creative genius—to manifest miracles on our behalf. Though the creation itself was completed in six days, we understand that God is still creatively blessing and moving in the earth to this day.

AT ROSH HASHANAH, WE HAVE AN OPPORTUNITY TO ACKNOWLEDGE GOD AS THE SUSTAINER OF EVERYTHING.

Throughout the year, we encounter numerous situations in which we must depend upon the Creator to come and intervene. We need Him to be victorious and continue to advance His kingdom. At Rosh Hashanah, we have an opportunity to acknowledge God as the Sustainer of everything that exists. As such, we anticipate seeing His handiwork throughout the year. We recognize that God will keep us, guide us, and protect us, from dangers seen and unseen.

At Rosh Hashanah, we also recognize that we depend upon God as our judge. We suffer from injustice, unfairness, and discrimination more times than we care to remember. In many cases, there is little or nothing we can do about it and we often walk around with a continual feeling of weakness because of it. But the God of Abraham, Isaac, and Jacob is omniscient and will not allow inequalities to go unpunished. (See Psalm 3; compare Psalm 1:6.)

RECOGNIZING OUR RESPONSIBILITY TO GOD

Rosh Hashanah gives us an opportunity to recognize God's expectations. God expects us to make His presence known in the world. Throughout the Scriptures, we see God using ordinary people to perform His will on earth. We must take ownership for our participation in God's work and fulfill our responsibility as believers to show forth His praise until Jesus comes again!

Rosh Hashanah helps us recognize that we are a critical part of the kingdom of God being manifest in our world. We must live with a mindset of desiring to reveal God and His mighty works to a lost and dying world.

ACKNOWLEDGING YHWH AS KING

The celebration of Rosh Hashanah is an acknowledgment of YHWH as king of the universe. At Rosh Hashanah, we recognize that He made the world and He is sovereign over it.

The Rosh Hashanah celebration begins with the blasting sound of the *shofar*, a specially crafted ram's horn that sounds like a high-pitched trumpet. It is a joyful and resounding sound, a sound of adoration and magnification.

In many ways, the blowing of the *shofar* on Rosh Hashanah signifies YHWH's coronation as king. (Compare Psalm 81:3.) Just as a king would march before his subjects, our YHWH is serenaded by His children with the blowing of the *shofar*. (See Leviticus 23:23–25.) Rosh Hashanah is a chance to remember repentance as we recognize the king of all!

3

YOM KIPPUR
AND GOD'S REMINDER THAT
WE'RE FORGIVEN

In the Jewish calendar, Yom Kippur is celebrated ten days after
Rosh Hashanah. (See Leviticus 23:26–27.) In many ways, Yom
Kippur, the Day of Atonement, is a commemoration of sin entering the world. (See Genesis 3.) But what makes Yom Kippur the
highest of holy days in the Jewish calendar is not the recognition of
sin, but the recognition of God's forgiveness!

UNDERSTANDING AND REMEMBERING FORGIVENESS

To understand the Day of Atonement, we must first examine
our view of forgiveness. What does forgiveness really mean and
do we ever truly practice it? One definition says forgiveness is "to
give up resentment of or claim to requital for... to grant relief from
payment of... to cease to feel resentment against (an offender)."

Now that's just the dictionary! If we stopped right there and went no further, you would still find it difficult to affirmatively answer the question, "Do you truly practice forgiveness?"

Most of the body of Christ does not truly embrace the most common definition of forgiveness. This therefore becomes one of the greatest tools of the enemy to distort and destroy relationships—to disrupt unity within the confines of the church.

Most of us can testify to not forgiving other Christians or not being forgiven by them. Right in the very environment where we recognize that forgiveness is the only reason why we even have access to God the Father, we fail at forgiveness. (Compare Ephesians 4:32; Colossians 3:12–13.) How distorted we have become! How is it that we believe we can walk in unforgiveness and still enjoy fellowship with the Father and fellowship in His church?

The very Hebrew word behind "atonement" essentially means "to cover." In this definition, we find the essence of the spiritual relationship between God and humanity. God could not deal with us without first forgiving us. His forgiveness allows us to avoid His wrath and instead enjoy God's bounty of blessings daily. (See Romans 1:16, 3:23–24.)

RECONCILIATION WITH GOD ALLOWS US TO EXPERIENCE FELLOWSHIP WITH HIM.

Reconciliation with God, by way of forgiveness, allows us to experience fellowship with Him. We cannot live perpetually with the confrontation of a holy God without forgiveness. We know ourselves to be sinners and we live with that sense of guilt or at least the reality of our failure. This is only highlighted when we are in the presence of holiness. This is why we can only truly be convicted of sin by God and not by another person. When Moses, Isaiah, and hundreds of others in the Scriptures are confronted with holiness, they fall to their knees or lay prostrate before the presence of the Lord. This happens because a person only truly realizes their failure when confronted with perfection. The Day of Atonement gives us such an opportunity.

WE SHOULD CELEBRATE THE DAY OF ATONEMENT

On the Day of Atonement, Israel was commanded to stop their work and commemorate forgiveness. (See Leviticus 23:28–32.) Leviticus 16:29 also says the Day of Atonement "*is to be a lasting ordinance*"—a statute practiced *forever*. While the Hebrew phrase here could be understood as referring to a long duration, there is no scriptural reason to stop practicing the Day of Atonement.

In my view, the Day of Atonement should not be canceled out by a new generation, a new worldview, or a contemporary approach to the faith. I believe this holy day is to be celebrated forever— period. We must just contextualize it differently in light of Christ's once and for all sacrifice.

On the Day of Atonement in ancient Israel, multiple sacrifices were made in recognition of sin and the need for purification. (See Leviticus 16.) But in our day, we can rejoice over the Lamb who was slain once and for all, for all *our* sins. (See Revelation 5:12; compare Isaiah 53:6–7.) In celebrating the Day of Atonement, we can expose the significance of our Savior's death: Jesus is the Lamb of God who takes away the sin of not only Israel but the whole world. (See John 1:29; compare Isaiah 53:10–12.)

The Day of Atonement also affords us the opportunity to reflect and fast.

[The LORD commanded Moses], "*This is to be a lasting ordinance for you: On the tenth day of the seventh month you must deny yourselves and not do any work—whether native-born or a foreigner residing among you—because on this day atonement will be made for you, to cleanse you. Then, before the* LORD*, you will be clean from all your sins. It is a day of sabbath rest, and you must deny yourselves."*

(Leviticus 16:29–31)

Self-denial during the Day of Atonement likely referred to fasting. Food and work are typically very distracting and consuming in our lives. By removing ourselves from these things at least once a year, we can focus on forgiveness. The Day of Atonement must be viewed as a Sabbath for us. For the Judeo-Christian, the Sabbath is a time of rest, worship, and fellowship. And the Day of Atonement is the most important Sabbath day.

4

ADAM, YOM KIPPUR, AND THE RECOGNITION OF SIN

The Day of Atonement, as a day that deals with sin, always brings us back to when sin came into the world—with Adam and Eve. (See Genesis 3.) Adam and Eve's story has much to teach us about God and the full meaning of forgiveness.

As I was exploring this topic, the Holy Spirit reminded me that Adam didn't pursue God, but God pursued Adam and drew close to him—despite Adam's disobedience. (See Genesis 3:8–10.) Adam had no way to rectify his relationship with God, yet the Father drew near to him with a plan to repair what Adam had ruined. While this is amazing, it is not the most astonishing part.

The most astonishing part is that throughout Genesis 3, neither Adam nor Eve ever apologized—yet God forgave them! Adam never said, "I'm sorry." He never took ownership of his disobedience. He never said, "Please forgive me, God." This point is what altered my perspective on forgiveness altogether. It changed the way I view the act and process of forgiveness.

NEITHER ADAM NOR EVE EVER APOLOGIZED—YET GOD FORGAVE THEM!

In the case of Adam and Eve, as in our lives, the Scriptures ring loud and clear:

> *When we were still powerless, Christ died for the ungodly. Very rarely will anyone die for a righteous person, though for a good person someone might possibly dare to die. But God demonstrates his own love for us in this: While we were **still** sinners, Christ died for us.*   (Romans 5:6–8)

We were *still* sinners. We were ungodly. We weren't apologetic, contrite, or repentant. We weren't looking for God or forgiveness. Yet prior to our admission of guilt, Christ had already provided the forgiveness and thus covered our sin.

When Adam sinned, it seems that he only knew guilt. His guilt was so overwhelming that in his view, there was no remedy. (See Genesis 3:10.) But then he is introduced to the concept of forgiveness. The discovery of forgiveness provided by YHWH revolutionized Adam's relationship with God the Father. Presumably, when God chose to let Adam live, it caused Adam to worship, adore, and appreciate God for the rest of his life. It endeared him to God like never before. God's forgiveness was not only a remedy for Adam and God, it was a remedy for him and Eve as well.

In order to fully digest this divine act and introduction of forgiveness, we have to understand Adam's position at the point of his disobedience. The enemy deceived Eve, not Adam. (See 1 Timothy

2:14.) In this regard, Adam can be considered the one to whom the full act of disobedience was ascribed. He committed the act of sinning in full knowledge, without deception being necessary. I am emphasizing this possibility because I want to change the way you categorize and understand "sin." For Adam to sin, he must first be completely disobedient. (See Genesis 3:17.) Sin is the byproduct of disobedience.

Once Adam was disobedient, he moved into a posture of sin. In this way, sin can be understood as a distortion of one's personality, perception, and comprehension. And this certainly aligns with the post-sin descriptions of Adam and Eve.

The Bible says they immediately saw each other through a distorted perspective of *nakedness*, despite the fact that they were unclothed previously and had no shame. (See Genesis 3:7–11, 21.) Once Adam and Eve moved into a distorted perception of everything God had made and called "good," they now saw it as bad and covered themselves.

But how is it that eating of the "tree of the knowledge of good and evil" changed Adam and Eve's personality, perception, and comprehension? It doesn't seem that this was a tree of categories—of understanding the difference between good and evil—despite the interpretations of many. Instead, it seems that when someone ate from the tree, they began to think of themselves as like God, with the ability to rely on their own discernment to distinguish between good and evil. (See Genesis 3:22.) But they did so without the understanding of God. When you decide what is good and what is evil, based on your own personal beliefs, surely distortion will be present.

After eating of the tree, Adam and Eve looked at each other through the distortion of sin, seeing one another as naked. What five minutes ago was good was now evil because they were now affected by *sin*. As a result of this distortion of personality, perception, and comprehension, they covered themselves and hid from God. Adam even seemed to deny Eve the dignity of being his spouse when he was confronted with the holiness of God. He told the Lord, *"The woman you put here with me—she gave me some fruit from the tree, and I ate it"* (Genesis 3:12). Yesterday, his relationship with Eve was good, but today, after disobedience, that same relationship was bad in Adam's eyes. Sin is a byproduct of disobedience that causes us to function in a strange and distorted manner, impacting our comprehension of everything around us.

SIN IS A BYPRODUCT OF DISOBEDIENCE THAT CAUSES US TO FUNCTION IN A STRANGE AND DISTORTED MANNER.

A CASE STUDY OF THE SIN-DISTORTION THEORY

Let's take one of the Ten Commandments and apply our new definition of sin to it. The Bible says, *"Thou shall not kill"* (Exodus 20:13). Another version may say *"you shall not murder."* In either case, we understand it to mean that we are forbidden to take the life of another human being. As simple as that commandment is, because of the distortion of sin, we justify murder under certain circumstances. Sometimes, we call it self-defense.

We may also wonder why Scripture tells us about times when God commanded someone to kill. For example, the prophet Samuel told Saul that God wanted him to "completely destroy" the Amalekites. But Saul allowed their king, Agag, and some of the Amalekites' animals to live. (See 1 Samuel 15:1–35.) He was then judged for his disobedience and lost the kingdom of Israel because of it. What we understand to be a commandment in Exodus was now overridden by the God's Word in the first book of Samuel.

Saul was commanded to kill in the context of war. But like Adam, he disobeyed. Essentially, Saul's actions were a byproduct of Adam's original choice; Saul believed that over and against God, he could differentiate between what was good and what was evil. This led to disobedience and the overall state of sin. Whether we are justifying killing—or in Saul's case, not killing despite God's command—we are under the distortion of sin. We take God's command and read it how we want. In Saul's case, Samuel said:

> Does the LORD delight in burnt offerings and sacrifices as much as in obeying the LORD? To obey is better than sacrifice, and to heed is better than the fat of rams. For rebellion is like the sin of divination, and arrogance like the evil of idolatry. Because you have rejected the word of the LORD, he has rejected you as king. (1 Samuel 15:22–23)

ADAM'S CHOICE CAUSED ALL OF US TO SUFFER FROM "SIN DISTORTION."

In reality, Adam's choice caused all of us to suffer from "sin distortion." It affects our personality, perception, and comprehension so drastically that unless God speaks to us on a daily and continual basis, we cannot distinguish what is good and what is evil. This is why Jesus, when tempted by the devil in the wilderness, said we must live by "every word" of God—or, more precisely, the *proceeding* words of God in Scripture. (See Matthew 4:4; compare Deuteronomy 8:3.)

Jesus's imagery is reminiscent of the experience of the people of Israel in the wilderness. Moses and the congregation needed the continual word of YHWH, which was manifest daily by the

movement of the cloud. (See Numbers 9:15–23.) God showed the
Israelites what they should do next, every day. In the same way, if
we are to move away from the effect of our sin nature, we can't do
so based our own interpretation of what is right and what is wrong.
We have to hear from God regularly and continuously, and follow
His direction. By walking in obedience, we can begin to realign
our minds and disconnect from the distortion of sin. Obedience
is the key!

CHANGING OUR PERSPECTIVE

If you can incorporate this definition of what sin really is into
your understanding of the divine act of forgiveness, then you can
better understand why Adam did not apologize, ask for forgiveness, or exhibit contrition. He was functioning under the distortion that sin brings. He was not himself anymore and his perception was off. He couldn't even fully comprehend what he had done.
Instead, he used the defense mechanisms of hiding and denial.
This makes it so obvious why Jesus said on the cross, *"Father, forgive them, for they do not know what they are doing"* (Luke 23:34). In
other words, sin has affected people so much that they can't even
comprehend the impact of their actions.

Yet, we expect people to be able to comprehend the hurt they
have inflicted upon us and apologize effectively. This is impossible! Remember, they are not themselves. Their personality is
skewed, their perception is twisted, and their comprehension is
perverted—and so it is with ours. Therefore, we are all in need of
divine forgiveness first, and then forgiveness from our brother or
sister.

THE ROLE OF THE DAY OF ATONEMENT

In light of all this, we can begin to comprehend the value
and significance of the Day of Atonement. There is so much to

be considered, remembered, and thankful for. On the Day of Atonement, we can feel incredibly close to God because He drew near to us—to reconcile and restore what had been severed through disobedience. In this, we can recognize the amazing act of love exhibited by Christ on the cross—innocence standing in for the guilty, perfection taking the place of the putrid, holiness being substituted for wickedness. From the standpoint of "the guilty," this is barely comprehensible, yet this is the type of forgiveness we have received from the Father through His Son.

There is nothing Adam could have done—or that we could do—to suffice such an egregious act of disobedience, so God did it for us. Still, the Day of Atonement is not merely a reminder of our sin, but rather of the great divine act of forgiveness. If the concept and reality of this kind of forgiveness is alive in us daily, it will enable us to deal with any offense that we experience.

When we think of what God did for us, we are to consider that He valued the relationship over the offense. If He had valued the offense over the relationship, Adam would not have experienced any more fellowship with Him. But when God came down in the cool of the day, it was a clear sign that the offense was not greater than the relationship and fellowship. (See Genesis 3:8.) What's amazing is that this is all the enemy was trying to do—his goal was to break the fellowship of God with Adam, Adam with Eve, and humanity with the earth. And he failed.

It is always the enemy's tactic to break fellowship because that is what happened to him when he was cast out of heaven. His fellowship was broken eternally; therefore, he desires to do the same thing with all of humankind. This is what we see all the time within nations, families, and churches. The enemy sees it and sets out to break it by any means necessary because he knows the power of unity and common purpose. This is why every church must begin again to highlight the power and purpose of forgiveness. Otherwise, over a period of time, the enemy will use this very issue to destroy the potential of the congregation or fellowship.

GOD IS NOT DISTRACTED FROM THE RELATIONSHIP OR FELLOWSHIP WITH US BECAUSE OF SIN.

What became even more powerful to me as I began to meditate on this thought is that the enemy uses disobedience and the sin nature to cause us to feel alienated from God. Yet God is not distracted from the relationship or fellowship with us because of sin. He never has been and He never will be.

This is possible because forgiveness was in place before Adam disobeyed and moved into sin. Jesus, the Lamb, was slain before *"the creation of the world"* (Revelation 13:8). This means that for our Father, Jesus was already slain and forgiveness was already in place before Adam committed his disobedient act. This is why sin was not a distraction for God. It was obviously a distraction for Adam and Eve, but not for the Almighty; He had already dealt with it before He made humanity.

This becomes the lesson for anyone who enters into a relationship with God—and it is a lesson for our relationships with other people. God entered the relationship prepared to forgive because the relationship had such great value for Him. In the same way, we must learn to enter our relationships with forgiveness for that person already intact and vice versa so when you find yourself in a situation that requires forgiveness, it is already in place—no apology needed. This is only possible when you are able to comprehend the forgiveness that you and I have received from the Father and when you value the relationship over the offense.

This concept is so powerful that even as you are reading, you may be reminiscing about past relationships that have been severed because of unforgiveness or the fact that you didn't value the relationship over the offense. What was the potential of that relationship? What could have come out of it had it remained? What purpose could it have served for you or the other person—or for persons unknown? What powerful things could you have accomplished together as a group? All of these questions and more need to be considered so we do not continue to give the offense greater value than the relationship.

Adam failed, but he still had a purpose. He still had power and potential to make things happen on God's behalf. When we enter a relationship, we must comprehend its power, potential, and purpose as well as be prepared to maintain that relationship when something goes wrong.

SIN MAKES US THINK WE ARE RIGHT WHEN WE ARE WRONG AND VICE VERSA.

The Day of Atonement, Yom Kippur, is all about relationship over offense. YHWH was fully prepared to deal with Adam as He is fully prepared to deal with us. The disobedience impacts us more than it impacts Him. He has a remedy for our disobedience; we are the ones who suffer from it with the byproduct of sin. We can't handle the effects of sin. It makes us think we are right when we are wrong. It makes us think we are wrong when we are right. Everything is so twisted by sin that we can't even think straight. However, forgiveness has become our remedy to that poisonous nature.

Live in the joy of your forgiveness and you will begin to live the life God designed for you. It will bring your mind back to its consciousness, bring your body back to normality, and bring your relationships back to their intended purpose.

PART TWO:

PRACTICING FORGIVENESS

5

HAVING A CONSCIOUSNESS OF FORGIVENESS

We have all found ourselves in situations that warrant for-giveness and will surely find ourselves in similar situations in the future. If you're a Christian, you must ask yourself, *What is required of me in this instance?* Is this just about hearing them out? Is it merely about me owning up to my participation in the mishap? Is it truly resolved when we shake hands or hug at the end of the conversation? Was it handled properly, emotionally? Did I let them get away with murder? Is it okay to walk away saying, "I'll never let that happen to me again"? How will this relationship continue in light of this indiscretion? These and other questions will present themselves in the privacy of your thoughts.

Most situations involving forgiveness are brought on by con-frontation, silence, or indifference. Afterward, we wait for the offending party to apologize and beg for forgiveness. Then we talk it out for a few minutes or a few hours. When this happens, we feel as if the problem was dealt with adequately and we can effectively move back into a relationship with that person or group.

This was illustrated perfectly in a Disney TV show I watched with my son. One of the family members disobeyed another family member by doing something they were specifically asked not to do. The offender then hid and ducked—trying not to get caught. Once caught and confronted, the offender realized the only option was to ask for forgiveness. Immediately, the offended said it was okay and that there was a solution. They hugged and moved on without a hitch. As I watched, I thought to myself, "This is the way the world thinks that forgiveness is administered."

This is also how the church practices forgiveness. But it's not biblical.

Forgiveness is best understood by how God handles it. Forgiveness is an act of God whereby He takes away the obstacle or barriers that separate people from His presence. The account of Adam and Eve after their disobedience shows this to be the case. (See Genesis 3:6–24.) God pursued Adam and Eve after their disobedience. God opens the way for reconciliation; the offended pursues the offender. It seems to me that God does this because Adam and Eve have no way of restoring their fellowship with Him. Since God's motivation is fellowship, He introduces forgiveness to His now distorted children so He can return to the fellowship they previously enjoyed.

JESUS SAYS THE ONE WHO IS FORGIVEN SHOULD HAVE A POSTURE OF FORGIVENESS.

God also offers forgiveness so people can fellowship with one another. Jesus emphasizes this concept in the Lord's Prayer when He says, *"Forgive us our debts, as we also have forgiven our debtors"* (Matthew 6:12). Jesus is saying that the one who is forgiven should have a posture of forgiveness—a person should give in the same manner that they have received. Being able to dispense forgiveness freely is a sign that someone has truly received and benefited from forgiveness.

Think back to a time when you might have offended someone. Did you apologize upfront? Like the offender in the Disney program, did you wait until you were confronted before offering any kind of contrition? Or like Adam in the garden, have you never apologized for the offense—perhaps even placed the blame on the other person?

It will often be no different with those who have wronged us. They will not be forthcoming with an apology, nor will they exhibit contrition unless they are found out. Maybe they will blame you or someone else. Yet Jesus taught us to forgive people the way we have been forgiven by God—no apology needed.

We should always keep in mind that God demonstrated His love for us while we were yet sinning. (See Romans 5:8.) God showed He loves us before we even thought to apologize.

God's version of forgiveness requires recognizing His forgiveness of us, while we were yet sinning, and thus offering others the same kind of forgiveness. What this essentially means is that when we're offended, we should humble ourselves by going to someone who has offended us and forgiving them, even before they have requested it. In doing so, you are essentially admitting in the midst of the offense, "I need you." Imagine that!

JESUS'S UNCONVENTIONAL VIEW OF FORGIVENESS

Jesus's view of forgiveness goes against conventional thinking. In the gospel of Matthew, Jesus masterfully lays out an argument that challenges the core concept of our relationship practices. (See Matthew 5:43–48.) It is common in our worldly practice to love those who love us, but Jesus switches all of that in the Sermon on the Mount. He tells us to love our enemies, bless those who curse us, be good to those who hate us, and pray for those who mistreat us. And if we thought this was the hard part, He follows up by saying, *"That you may be children of your Father in heaven"* (verse 45).

JESUS ASKS US NOT ONLY TO ACCEPT ABUSE FROM ANOTHER, BUT TO BE NICE IN RETURN.

When you think about it, this is incredible. Not only is He asking us to accept the abuse that another is imposing on us, He is also asking us to be nice in return. This is where even the most devout Christian will have difficulty. However, what Jesus asks of us is not just so that we are humbled—nor is He suggesting we be abused in a frivolous sense. Living by Jesus's teaching is how we can demonstrate that we are in relationship with the Father. What Jesus suggests we do is what God does all the time and if you say you are His son or daughter, then you must do the same.

Now most of us will still find this to be just a little beyond our pay grade, but He further explains our need to follow this paradigm, saying the Father *"causes his sun to rise on the evil and the good, and sends rain on the righteous and the unrighteous"* (Matthew 5:45). How powerful is that? We don't have God's infinite knowledge and understanding, which means we judge who is good and who is evil based on a very limited amount of information. Yet God—who has all of the information and can properly judge the just from the unjust—still allows both sun and rain to fall on all of us without prejudice. If God can do this, then certainly we can emulate Him by being nice to those who we perceive as being not nice to us.

Jesus continues the lesson with one more point about departing from worldly practices and taking on the posture of our Father in heaven. He says if you only love those who love you, there is no reward. So by implication, a reward is connected to loving, blessing, being good, and praying for those who mistreat you. Jesus says if you don't do this, you are the same as the world. To distinguish yourself from worldly practice, you must disassociate yourself from the world in your deeds.

Therefore, these acts of humility, forgiveness, and kindness toward your brother or sister—regardless of how ungodly he or she may treat you—are directly related to how your Father deals with you. However, none of these actions would be possible if forgiveness was not in place prior to the offenses. When Jesus offers this teaching, He is functioning from the definition of forgiveness as a verb, not merely a noun. You cannot say you forgive if there is no corresponding action to go along with that statement. There should be a consciousness of forgiveness on the part of the offended.

RETHINKING "FORGIVE AND FORGET"

If I think of forgiveness as an action I must take, then I cannot simply forgive and forget; I have to forgive and remember. I must remember the forgiveness.

Let me explain what I mean and why I believe in this principle. When I am offended, I feel the effects of that action. My responsibility now, according to Scripture, is to forgive that person in my heart. I must then let them know that I suffered an offense from them and show, by some action, that forgiveness has been applied to the situation.

In this regard, God's actions in the garden of Eden speak volumes. Notice that God was the offended. He went to Adam and Eve as they are hiding out from Him to let them know their actions offended Him. Then—by the act of killing innocent animals and using their skins to make clothing for Adam and Eve—He showed them that they were forgiven. (See Genesis 3:8–9, 21.) Adam and Eve had only defended themselves, passed the blame to one another, and missed the chance to apologize. Yet God placed the garments of skin on them. He forgave, but this does not mean He forgot. Every time He saw them from this point forward, He would see the clothing He made for them and thus remember the forgiveness He had applied.

When we actively forgive a person, every time we see them, we will remember that we forgave them. By taking the action of forgiveness, we move into a posture of forgiveness toward the offender. This causes us to remember the forgiveness, not the offense. The revelation of this is awesome and practical. It is also based in truth: We know that whenever our heavenly Father looks at us, He sees the blood of His Son and remembers that we are forgiven. *"As far as the east is from the west, so far has he removed our transgressions from us"* (Psalm 103:12). The transgression is removed because the forgiveness has been actively applied.

When we say we can forgive but not forget, it is because we forgave based upon an apology, not based upon *our* act of forgiveness. Apologies don't make things better; forgiveness makes things better.

THE CONSCIOUSNESS OF FORGIVENESS

In every scenario that Jesus outlines in Matthew 5:43–48, it is understood that we are not dealing with people who are apologetic. Jesus refers to people who are enemies, those who curse you or hate you, and those who are spiteful and take an opportunity to persecute you. We get no sense of remorse or contrition on their part. Thus Jesus is asking us to match what He and the Father have done—to function from a posture of forgiveness. This means that forgiveness is not an event-motivated state of mind; it is a conscious and constant state of mind motivated by the way our Father in heaven functions all the time with us. This being the case, we must transcend the way the world functions in this area and mimic our Father.

> FORGIVENESS IS A CONSCIOUS AND CONSTANT STATE OF MIND MOTIVATED BY THE WAY OUR FATHER IN HEAVEN FUNCTIONS.

But there is still one more very important part of this consciousness that must be considered. At the end of Jesus's teaching on forgiveness, He says if we practice forgiveness in this fashion, *"you shall be perfect, just as your Father in heaven is perfect"* (Matthew 5:48 NKJV). The implication is that the Father expects us to strive for and grow to a particular level of maturity that authenticates our relationship with Him. This relationship is not authenticated by religious practices, as institutionalized religion would have us believe. Proof that we are sons and daughters of the Father is best realized when we exhibit His character in the most unsavory of situations. When we see this as a goal for our spiritual walk—and then begin to see it manifest in our daily lives—we are, at that point, walking in perfection.

HOW JESUS PRACTICED CONSCIOUS FORGIVENESS

When Jesus walked the earth, He understood the need to have a consciousness of forgiveness and was always prepared to forgive. Watch Jesus in Matthew 9:1–8 as He deals with a paralytic man carried to Him on a mat. Because of His consciousness, the first thing Jesus says to the man is, "*Take heart, son; your sins are forgiven*" (Matthew 9:2). There is no apology or acknowledgment of any guilt or failure on the part of the paralytic. However, Jesus seems to indicate that his condition is related to unforgiven sin. We don't look at abnormalities, illnesses, and diseases this way, but in some cases, this is why people remain sick. The condition of sin had distorted the man's body; he was suffering from his body functioning abnormally because he needed this distortion to be forgiven. Jesus comes along and tells him, "On behalf of the Father, your sins are released from you," and immediately, the man's circumstances change. Interestingly, it is possible for an illness to be related to our psychological state. Some heart attacks and ulcers are examples of this. Presumably, if someone had forgiven the man at the point of his transgression, he would not have suffered from the physical ailment at all.

A related story is found in John 8:1–12. In this story, the scribes and Pharisees confront Jesus about a woman they supposedly caught in the act of adultery. I'm not sure if this was a setup, since the man is nowhere to be found, but I'm sure she wasn't committing the act by herself. The challenge put upon Jesus is, "How should she be dealt with in light of the law of Moses?" Jesus is again conscious of her need to be forgiven. He does not respond verbally to their query; instead, He stoops down and writes on the ground with His finger. My speculation about what He wrote is that it must not have been offensive since the crowd remains when He stands up again. Maybe He simply confirmed their accusation by inscribing the law in the dirt. He states the criteria whereby the stoning may commence—*"Let any one of you who is without sin be the first to throw a stone at her"* (John 8:7)—then He stoops down and writes some more. The crowd was then convicted by their own conscience and everyone leaves, one by one, beginning with the oldest.

The case of the woman caught in adultery teaches us a few things. First, the more religious you are, the less conscious of forgiveness you may be. It is religious people who honor the letter of the law, but not the spirit of the law. (See Romans 8:2; compare Galatians 5:18.) It is obviously not God's desire to stone the adulterer any more than it is His desire to kill the liar. However, when you are driven by the rigidity of the law and not the spirit of love, you are deluded into believing you have been left to execute judgment on God's behalf. These religious zealots needed a conscience check and they got one that day from the Christ.

Secondly, I believe that Jesus, upon stooping down the second time, could very well have been writing the sins, dates, times, and names of those standing around Him, so as to convict them. Whatever He did, it caused them to relax their religious viewpoint and abandon their stones, essentially forcing them to forgive.

This tends to be the case most often in the world today. We don't forgive because it comes naturally; we forgive because we are reminded of our own failures and thus realize the penalty we are attempting to impose upon someone else could also be imposed upon us. They all walked away, starting with the oldest, signifying that no one felt justified to punish this woman any longer. In essence, the persecutors became conscious of forgiveness.

What's absolutely amazing about this story is that the one who could have legitimately began the stoning—Jesus—chose instead to forgive. Again, this reiterates that Jesus lived with the consciousness of forgiveness at all times.

Additionally, this woman neither apologizes nor asks for forgiveness, yet she leaves having her sins forgiven and her nature forever changed by the experience. If we could be so conscious of a person's need to be forgiven—and offer it as a substitute for judgment—how many lives would be transformed by that act of love and kindness? It is the greatest gift any human can give or receive from another. It is redemptive, kind, restorative, virtuous, and life-giving. More people are damaged and live in perpetual suffering from unforgiven sin than we could ever imagine. We each live with this damage. Just being conscious of it could be the key to reversing the trend.

MORE PEOPLE ARE DAMAGED FROM UNFORGIVEN SIN THAN WE COULD EVER IMAGINE.

We also see the consciousness of forgiveness in Luke 7:36–50 when Simon invites Jesus over for a dinner with other prominent, religious leaders. (Compare Matthew 26:6–13.) I imagine that the house was full of servants catering to Simon's high-class Pharisee friends. Each of the Pharisees was probably admiring the fine things around them and looking for the most important seat. Maybe there was some initial conversation about the activities of the temple or what was coming up on the Jewish calendar. Then just before the bread and oil come out, a woman who heard that Jesus was at the table makes her way from the outer fringes to a little space right behind Jesus. Immediately, everyone recognizes her as a sinner from that town. A strange silence comes over the room as she kneels down, her eyes to the ground to avoid eye contact with any of the religious leaders. Out of her pocket comes an alabaster flask of fragrant oil. A servant looks at Simon to see if he will give the cue to throw her out. Simon doesn't move.

Suddenly, the sound of sniffling begins to emanate from beneath the long black mane that now screens the woman's face. The sniffling escalates into tears that flow like a freshwater spring for the next several minutes. There is enough water to saturate Jesus's feet. No compassion is produced in the room, just judgment and disdain—she's taking attention away from their high-level religious dinner. They're hoping this whole episode will be over quickly. Jesus is not in the least bit disturbed by the interruption. Now her long beautiful hair is being used as a towel, to gently pat his tired, weary feet.

The woman then opens the flask of scented oil and a powerful essence of spices fills the room—enough to overwhelm the aroma of freshly cooked food. She begins the final step by massaging the oil into his feet.

Knowing Simon's thoughts, Jesus says, "*Simon, I have something to tell you*" (Luke 7:40). Simon is ready to hear the lesson. Jesus tells a story of two debtors who owed a creditor. One debtor owed the equivalent of five hundred days' wages and the other fifty days' wages. When the creditor called in the loans, neither could pay, so the creditor forgave them both. Jesus then asks a rhetorical question, "*Which of them will love him more?*" (verse 42). Simon answers that it will be the one who owed the most money. Jesus says, "*You have judged correctly*" (verse 43). Jesus then offers an indictment on Simon's attitude, comparing his poor hospitality to the woman's actions. (See Luke 7:44–47.)

Jesus's comment to Simon that he has judged correctly seems to be an allusion to the fact that Simon and the others at the table have been judging the woman. This is exactly where most people stand in light of someone else's faults and shortcomings—in judgment. When we have a posture of judgment, it is impossible to possess a consciousness of forgiveness. This is exactly why so many of our relationships are fragmented and marginalized. For some reason, we just don't seem to possess the humility or introspection to realize that we are no better than the person we are judging. Jesus knows that most of the people in the room have the wrong perspective of the woman and of themselves. And that is the underlying problem.

Jesus does not justify the woman's "many sins." There is no getting around the fact that she messed up. Her precise sins are unknown to us, but everyone in the town apparently knew about them. But that's not Jesus's point. For Jesus, everyone around the table has the same disposition for sin. Everyone there has a soul that is distorted and driven by an appetite. They have all messed up and have lived a repugnant lifestyle, whether they or anyone else knows it or not. Jesus is the only person there who has the capacity to judge rightly and He still doesn't do it. He chooses to function from a consciousness of forgiveness because He knows that anyone and everyone is redeemable. Hallelujah! If it were left up to my critics, my enemies, or even my shortsighted friends, I would be doomed to the prison of unforgiveness, but thankfully, God has freely offered me forgiveness.

Knowing what He does, Jesus tells this little parable about the debtors to see if He can override the religious piety around the table and move everyone to introspection and humility. The point here is that everyone owes a debt to the master, but not everyone perceives how much they owe. In the woman's case, she realized she had a tremendous amount of sin that needed to be forgiven. She was also acutely aware of who had the power to forgive her, which is an even stronger indictment against those sitting at the table. They would never approach Jesus to request the forgiveness of their sins. However, the woman discerns who Jesus is and it causes her to spring into action—regardless of how she may be construed—because she knows she needs forgiveness.

By comparing a humble sinner to a haughty religious community, Jesus underscores the difference in their practice and posture. He essentially says to Simon, "When I came into your house, you were not hospitable." Simon was so arrogant and unforgiven (sin distorted) that basic courtesies shown to any guest, much less a rabbi, were not shown to Jesus. Simon expected Jesus to sit there with dirty feet. Simon did not give Jesus a proper greeting. Simon did not anoint Jesus with perfumed oil to honor Him and enhance His dinner experience. This makes me wonder, what was wrong with Simon? It also makes us wonder what is wrong with some people in the church.

What really captures my attention in this passage is the dramatic way the woman tended to Jesus's needs—in another's house no less. Instead of water from a pitcher drawn from a well, she uses water from her eyes squeezed out of her longing soul. Instead of using the household towel hanging at the doorway entrance to dry Jesus's feet, she uses the glory of her womanhood—her silky tresses—to gently pat the tears from His toes. Instead of the common Jewish greeting of a kiss on the cheek, as a sign of friendship and respect, she lowered her lips and tenderly kissed His feet over and over again with a sensitivity that was unnerving. Lastly, a little oil for Jesus's head would have been a minimal indication of Simon's appreciation for Jesus's attendance. Simon doesn't provide this, but the woman dramatically anoints Jesus.

Yet despite all of this, we know that when you describe a spiritual principle to a religious person, they tend to miss the point, as Simon seems to do. Jesus makes it very clear that the woman's sins, which are many, are forgiven and this forgiveness is based upon how much she has exhibited love and faith—acknowledging her sins in the process. Now the opposite is true for those who do not perceive that they have a sin problem. They tend to love less because they think their sins are less. What a sad reality this is for so many shortsighted people who struggle to forgive others of their faults. It doesn't mean that they don't have a multitude of sins; it just means they have ceased to recognize them.

SIN IS SO DISTORTING, IT CAUSES YOU TO SEE YOURSELF AS SINNING LESS THAN OTHERS.

Sin is so distorting, it actually causes you to see yourself as sinning less than others. When you don't recognize your sins, it becomes difficult to have a consciousness of forgiveness. When Jesus turns to the woman and says her sins are forgiven, the religious in the room are beside themselves. It's almost as if they don't believe that certain people should be afforded this luxury. Furthermore, they wonder who Jesus is to offer such graciousness to such an unredeemable individual.

I hope that when we internalize the implications of this story—and apply it to our daily Christian experience—we can move away from the terrible attitude of judgment and haughtiness, which has ruined many relationships. Let us move toward a humility based upon a consciousness of forgiveness, recognizing that we are forgiven and others need to receive what has been so graciously bestowed upon us. This woman's faithful, risky actions caused her to walk out of Simon's house with her salvation secured.

Jesus was so conscious of our need for forgiveness that even from the cross, He uttered the words that seemed outrageous to nonbelieving onlookers: *"Father, forgive them, for they do not know what they are doing"* (Luke 23:34). This speaks directly to Jesus's spirituality—He does as His Father would do. (Compare Matthew 5:44–45.)

Most people who hurt us don't know what they are doing. Likewise, we don't really know what we are doing to the people we hurt. If we knew, would we behave differently? Maybe not. After all, sin has distorted us. This is why we all need forgiveness and we all need to be conscious of forgiveness. We need to move from a place of judgment and religiosity to a posture of grace and forgiveness.

6

HOW MANY TIMES SHOULD I FORGIVE?

How many times should I forgive?" In all of my days in the church and Christianity, I have heard this question debated. Arguments surrounding this question usually have to do with the temperament of the human spirit and psyche. Everyone knows and realizes there is a limit to how much one person can take. We all attest to it to one degree or another. Some people have a high tolerance for pain, injury, or abuse; others may not be able to get through one grievance without serious difficulty. There is also a certain absurdity that goes along with allowing someone to take advantage of you continuously, without some type of retaliation or consequence exacted. For this reason, we often justify our inability to continue to forgive a person who repeatedly wrongs us.

Peter once asked Jesus, *"Lord, how many times shall I forgive my brother or sister who sins against me? Up to seven times?"* (Matthew 18:21). In light of the revelation that I must live with a consciousness of forgiveness, I wonder if we can answer Peter's question with, "How many times would you like to be forgiven?" This is essentially what Jesus says when He tells Peter he must forgive seventy-seven times or seventy times seven, depending on the translation. (See Matthew 18:22.) Jesus then tells a parable that illustrates how being forgiven should create a spirit of reciprocity—it should cause us to forgive others, as we have been forgiven. (See Matthew 18:23–35.)

If you look at the problem of forgiving others this way, the entire equation is altered. I no longer forgive based upon my personal tolerance level for how many times I am willing to be wronged. Instead, I forgive based upon how many times I would like God to forgive me. This altered perspective automatically adjusts our tolerance level for forgiving others.

PETER'S QUESTION AND GREATNESS IN THE KINGDOM

To fully understand Peter's question about forgiveness, we must understand it in the context of the gospel of Matthew, much of which revolves around Jesus's sermons. They are punctuated by phrases like "and Jesus answered and said" and "when Jesus had finished these sayings." In between these phrases, we regularly find Jesus's answer or response to a question or situation. Peter's question comes after one of these sermons. The sermon began with the question, "*Who, then, is the greatest in the kingdom of heaven?*" (Matthew 18:1).

This question prompts Jesus to call a little child to come to Him to help Him make a significant point. (See Matthew 18:2–4.) As the child stands before the inquisitive group, Jesus says you can't enter the kingdom of heaven unless you change and become like little children. What's frightening is that the disciples are asking about becoming great in the kingdom, yet Jesus is suggesting that they are not even in the kingdom yet. If they were already in the kingdom, they would not be asking about greatness in the presence of the greatest one there. Thus Jesus must start by helping them see how to get into the kingdom. Notably, entry into the kingdom begins with conversion or a changed mind. In other words, if you are concerned with greatness and being noteworthy, then you must change that thought process and others to embrace the kingdom.

IF YOU ARE CONCERNED WITH GREATNESS, YOU CANNOT EMBRACE THE KINGDOM OF HEAVEN.

Second, the nature of a child is humility and this is also a necessary characteristic of anyone who wishes to gain entry into the kingdom. Again, the disciples' question speaks to their lack of humility. However, the posture of humility that Jesus speaks of goes beyond our typical understanding, which is why He uses the reference of a little child. Children are humble largely due to their dependence and vulnerability.

Children are basically subject to, and dependent upon, their parents for all of their provisions at the early stages of life. Due to this dependence, there is no way a little child can feel proud or great on their own. Children have nothing to boast about at all because everything they enjoy is provided by someone greater than themselves. In addition, unlike adults, children have no choice but to be dependent. So greatness in the kingdom is directly related to a willingness to be dependent upon others, which is typically not found in someone who lacks humility.

While looking at this little child, we see vulnerability in a dramatic way. Since children don't fully control anything in their lives, they are vulnerable to anything that happens in the lives of their parents. If the parents are struggling financially or angry, the child also suffers. If the parents are brilliant, the child is impacted by their intellect. Anyone who lives under the shadow of someone else's life choices rarely claims any accomplishment of their own; they are typically very humble. It is in this context that Jesus describes the need to be converted and become as a little child—emulating that dependence and vulnerability in order to enter His kingdom. This is how Jesus defines greatness in the kingdom of heaven, but Jesus doesn't end His answer there. He goes on to note that whoever receives a vulnerable little child receives Him. (See Matthew 18:5.)

Jesus then turns to the wider point that you must be very careful how you deal with someone who has become so dependent and vulnerable—to the point of humility—because you don't want it said that you took advantage of them or hurt them. (See Matthew 18:6.) It is in this context that Jesus introduces the topic of things that cause people to stumble. (See Matthew 18:7–9.) Jesus is essentially saying that if you want to be great in the kingdom, then you will put yourself in a position to be tempted and offended and you need to be aware of things that will cause you to stumble.

Jesus brings stumbling blocks or offenses into the conversation about greatness because there is a need to protect those who are as humble as little children. This protection comes by way of a warning. Since those who are in the kingdom are vulnerable, Jesus warns the disciples that it would be better for them to drown in the sea than to cause someone else to sin. At a glance, this would seem to be just a little dramatic. However, what Jesus is speaking of here is not a simple offense—He is speaking of leading another into sin.

Jesus says little children have angels who communicate with God, face to face—and these angels will speak to the Father on their behalf if anyone causes them to sin! (See Matthew 18:10.)

If anyone decides to still lead others astray under these circumstances, they will probably reap some harsh judgment from the Most High.

By way of a parable, Jesus takes a moment to let His audience know that if someone gets off course and strays away from the flock, He will leave the flock and go find the one led astray. (See Matthew 18:11–14.) He is not willing for any to be lost. We still have not reached the answer to Peter's question about how many times he should forgive someone, but we are gleaning his reasons for asking it.

Since those who cause us to stumble are often those who offend us, Jesus now introduces a kingdom perspective on how to deal with someone who offends us. (See Matthew 18:15–17; compare with Matthew 7:1–5.) Jesus says the first step is a one-on-one attempt to get the offending brother to repent from his ways. If this doesn't work, He tells us to include some witnesses, but not the whole church. Finally, if the brother still doesn't hear you, then and only then should the entire church challenge him. Keep in mind that all of these efforts should be done with the desire to redeem the offending brother, not punish him. Everyone is redeemable.

When I look at the process Jesus outlines here, I am reminded how unfortunate it is that in most of my church experience, the process has been just the opposite. Typically, if someone was found in an offense or the instigator of a scandal, in a very clandestine way, the whole church knew about it in a heartbeat. Afterward, some part of the leadership would attempt to redeem the person. Finally, the parties involved would try to talk it out. It's strange how we have ignored the scriptural process laid out by Jesus; the process we have substituted shows no motivation for redemption. Instead, it seems like the motivation is to condemn and judge, and then make a weak attempt at so-called restoration. As a result, the church and several innocent bystanders become collateral damage.

This has been so commonplace in my experience that I'm sure that when many look at the biblical prescription, it almost seems foreign.

At this point in Matthew's gospel, we've nearly reached Peter's highly rational question. Before it occurs, however, Jesus offers a curious statement. I've heard this particular statement of Jesus quoted over and over in church settings, across denominational and cultural lines, yet I don't think we have used it appropriately or contextually. As Jesus continues to break down how to deal with a belligerent brother, He sums up the process by saying:

> *Truly I tell you, whatever you bind on earth will be bound in heaven, and whatever you loose on earth will be loosed in heaven. Again, truly I tell you that if two of you on earth agree about anything they ask for, it will be done for them by my Father in heaven. For where two or three gather in my name, there am I with them.* (Matthew 18:18–20)

This statement—found in the midst of Jesus's teachings on how to deal with a fallen brother's sin—caused great concern and curiosity for me because I knew the way I had heard the verse used did not fit the context Jesus spoke it in. So what is Jesus talking about? It's not prayer, warfare, or manipulating the will of God. So what is it?

WE POSSESS THE POWER TO RELEASE A PERSON FROM THEIR OFFENSE OR RETAIN THE OFFENSE.

In a way that we don't properly comprehend, we possess the power to release a person from their offense or retain the offense against that person. Let me explain by using a familiar story from the Old Testament. In Genesis 32–33, we find the account of Jacob preparing to meet Esau after many years of separation. The last time Jacob saw his twin brother, he had just manipulated him out of his birthright and his blessing. (See Genesis 27:41–45.) When Jacob left their home, he knew Esau wanted to kill him because of what he had done. With this in mind, Esau bound that offense and did not forgive Jacob. So all of Jacob's actions are now based upon being bound to his offense. If Esau had released Jacob of the offense, Jacob would not have feared for his life, fled his father's house, or ended up living with Laban for over fourteen years. (Note: I do not discount God's sovereignty in all of this. Esau binding Jacob to his offense was the cause of subsequent events that may not have necessarily happened if Esau had released him immediately.)

Still bound to his offense fourteen years later, Jacob is full of fear and dread as he prepares to face his brother again. Therefore, prior to his arrival, he sends gifts and family members to Esau to appease him and possibly spare himself the consequences of his actions—just in case there is some venom still present in his brother's heart.

You and I both know how this feels, from either end of the equation; the feelings here resonate. We have all been in situations where a lingering, unresolved, or unforgiven offense impacts not only our actions, but also how we feel about an interaction. In these moments, there is no telling how the person we offended will treat us or if they will retaliate for a former offense. This feeling has everything to do with the power to release or retain offenses. When a sin or offense is released, the person knows they are freed of the consequences of their actions and they can function normally in their interactions with you. When a sin or offense is retained, they know that when they see you again, their normal interactions with you will be complicated by the remembrance of the offense.

It seems to me that what Jesus is saying is that if you take the proper steps with a brother or sister—as it relates to making them aware of the offense, as described in Matthew 18:16–19—then and only then can you decide to either bind the person to the offense or release them from it. In light of this, it seems that Jesus is indicating that God, in some way, acknowledges the conclusion of the church when it binds or loosens an offense. (Compare Matthew 16:19; John 20:23.)

HOW OFTEN SHOULD WE FORGIVE?

It is after Jesus's lengthy monologue about greatness in the kingdom of heaven—and confronting someone who has wronged you—that Peter asks the question, *"Lord, how many times shall I forgive my brother or sister who sins against me? Up to seven times?"* (Matthew 18:21).

It seems like Peter is struggling with the feeling that he will be taken advantage of, be abused, or reach his point of maximum tolerance and be unable to obey Jesus's teaching. But remember, the real issue here is the original question that prompted Jesus's monologue: *"Who, then, is the greatest in the kingdom of heaven?"* (Matthew 18:1). Thus, Jesus is making the point that an essential attribute of members of the kingdom, and greatness in the kingdom, is the ability to forgive! Greatness is directly correlated to forgiveness. This quality not only represents your maturity in the kingdom, but also your closeness to the One who forgave you—God Himself.

Let's take a closer look at Peter's intriguing question. First, we must acknowledge it suggests a certain posture of haughtiness because it implies that someone else would not be required to do the same thing for Peter. It seems he thinks of himself as the one who must forgive others, not the other way around. Second, Peter attempts to look generous, noting he would forgive up to seven times. This again suggests a certain level of arrogance. (Compare Luke 17:4.)

Jesus answers Peter, "*I tell you, not seven times, but seventy-seven times*" (Matthew 18:22). In another translation, Jesus says, "*I do not say to you, up to seven times, but up to seventy times seven*" (Matthew 18:22 NKJV).

At this point, I'm sure Peter is sorry that he even opened his mouth.

Jesus's answer is astounding. We can comprehend Peter's number, but Jesus's answer takes it to another level—it is incomprehensible. Why doesn't Jesus give a number that is reasonable? Why doesn't He give a number we can work with? Doesn't He know how difficult it will be to manage this many offenses from just one person—seventy-seven of them, or maybe four hundred and ninety? Doesn't He know that we can only tolerate other people wronging us a certain number of times? Doesn't He have a heart for the one who is being abused and taken advantage of? Doesn't He know it will be impossible for us to keep track of this many offenses, even if it's the smaller number?

But maybe the absurdity of Jesus's response is the point.

Peter's very question suggests that he desires to eventually reach a position where he will no longer have to forgive. At some point, Peter thinks, he should be able to stop forgiving an offending brother. He doesn't realize he is actually positioning himself to become unforgiving. Jesus knows if this were to happen, it would harm Peter more than the person who offended him. In essence, Peter is actually asking Jesus, "At what point can I become bound by a spirit of unforgiveness? At what point can I allow bitterness to enter in, as a result of my unforgiveness?" Of course, it doesn't sound this way as he poses the question, but this is essentially what he's asking.

JESUS ASKS US TO STRETCH OUR TOLERANCE FOR OFFENSES BEYOND MEASURE.

As a result of the underlying assumptions behind Peter's question, Jesus asks Peter to stretch his tolerance for offenses beyond measure; He doesn't want Peter to be bound by a spirit of unforgiveness. It is critical for us to comprehend this. When it comes to forgiving, we tend to be more concerned with a person getting away with an offense than ourselves being bound by unforgiveness. We must value our freedom from bondage and allow the Holy Spirit to deal with the offender.

Jesus is still dealing with the question of who is the greatest in the kingdom. He now applies forgiveness to the kingdom by offering a parable. Jesus tells us about a king and a servant who are both owed money:

Therefore, the kingdom of heaven is like a king who wanted to settle accounts with his servants. As he began the settlement, a man who owed him ten thousand bags of gold was brought to him. Since he was not able to pay, the master ordered that he and his wife and his children and all that he had be sold to repay the debt. At this the servant fell on his knees before him. "Be patient with me," he begged, "and I will pay back everything." The servant's master took pity on him, canceled the debt and let him go. But when that servant went out, he found one of his fellow servants who owed him a hundred silver coins. He grabbed him and began to choke him. "Pay back what you owe me!" he demanded. His fellow servant fell

to his knees and begged him, "Be patient with me, and I will
pay it back." But he refused. Instead, he went off and had the
man thrown into prison until he could pay the debt.

(Matthew 18:23–30)

At this point, the moral of the story can be ascertained: you
should show the same compassion to others that has been shown
to you. But there's more to this parable.

Let's go back to the beginning of the parable for a moment.
Notice Peter's question focuses on an offense from one *brother*
to another *brother*. But Jesus's parable focuses on a king and his
subjects. This is not by accident. This is designed as imagery of
the kingdom; it deals with the authority of the king and his final
judgment. This parable shows how the kingdom operates. Jesus
talks about how a king deals with his subjects to show Peter how
to deal with his brother. In other words, the way the king, who is
above you, deals with you is the same way you must deal with your
brother, who is on the same level as you. Additionally, the way you
deal with your brother is the way the king will deal with you.

In the parable, the king initially wants the servant to pay his
debt in full. The debt in question is no small matter; it's equal to
about 150,000 years' worth of wages—an absurd amount, a debt
that is impossible to repay.

When the king realizes the man cannot pay him, he threatens
him with devastating consequences. He commands that the man
and his family be sold. They would be slaves for the rest of their
lives. Additionally, all of their possessions would be sold to recoup
as much of the debt as possible.

Faced with such dire consequences, the man becomes desper-
ate to save himself, his family, and his possessions. He pleads with
the king and asks for patience because he will pay it all. Patience—
are you kidding me!? What kind of gift of gab did this guy possess?

The debt is *insurmountable.* Patience has nothing to do with it; it simply cannot be done.

In an amazing turn of events and change of heart, instead of selling the man and his family into slavery, placing him in prison, or punishing him by any other number of devastating alternatives, the king decides to *forgive* the debt! This is stunning mainly because the man never asked for forgiveness! This is life-changing and mind-altering. This is deliverance. This is freedom. This is a new chance at life. This is more than the man could have ever imagined. He walked in the door trying to negotiate the terms of a life-long debt sentence and walked out with no debt at all. Technically, he became wealthy in a split-second just by one act of forgiveness. He is a changed man and a new man.

Or is he?

I can imagine the man rejoicing as he's walking down the street. He's telling everyone how he and his family have been spared from bondage. The story is mesmerizing to those who hear it. What kind of king forgives that kind of debt? The wife is relieved, the kids are excited—daddy is not stressed out anymore. The house will be at peace. No more ducking and hiding from those they owe money to; life is new. You can imagine the man saying, "This is a day to remember. Mark the calendar. Let's celebrate this day every year as long as we live. Let's have a feast. Let's eat, drink, and be merry for the rest of our lives. The debt that was impossible to pay is forgiven!"

However, on his way home, the man finds a *fellow* servant who owes him a relatively insignificant sum—about a hundred days' wages. Upon seeing his fellow servant, the man immediately challenges the servant to pay it all. When he realizes the man cannot pay, he moves to violence without hesitation. With his hands around the servant's throat, he demands that the debt be paid without delay.

The fellow servant, using the same language that the forgiven man used earlier, asks for patience because indeed he will pay it all. It's amazing that hearing these same words that he himself said to the king doesn't trigger something in this guy's mind to cause him to think back to the king's generosity and his own forgiveness. How could this be? How could someone be so callous and thoughtless? The forgiveness he just received has not affected his soul the way it should have.

With such a small amount at stake, I'm sure the fellow servant is not lying either. This very small amount could be paid in a short amount of time, perhaps by borrowing from a friend. However, the man who just recently received incredibly generous forgiveness from the king is merciless. Despite the other servant begging for patience, the relationship dynamics do not change; the first servant does not offer forgiveness or mercy.

This is a direct contrast to the king. It seems forgiveness was already a part of the king's posture. Thus he was able to offer forgiveness even when it wasn't requested. But in the case of the servant-to-servant relationship, forgiveness was not a part of the lender's character, which makes him incapable of offering even leniency to his fellow servant—even after the latter begs for patience.

THE IMPORTANCE OF HAVING CAPACITY TO FORGIVE

When we understand that forgiveness is a posture—not an action that is event-driven or apology-motivated—we will save ourselves from pain and disappointment. This should change our behavior altogether. In the past, we did not recognize this, so we struggled to forgive. Depending on how deep the offense was, we would either release it immediately or bind the offense to the offender until their actions justified our forgiveness. Now, with this revelation in mind, we realize we must walk continuously in a posture of forgiveness, so that regardless of the offense, we are fully prepared to forgive.

Jesus's parable about forgiveness illustrates how the absence of a forgiving spirit can make a man feel justified in his actions toward another. This is the argument or position we most often find in an unforgiving person. They stand unapologetically and explain why they won't budge one bit. They feel justified and normally you cannot talk them out of their position. This is such a dangerous place to be in, especially if you claim to be a Christian. There is no justification for being unforgiving once you've been forgiven.

FORGIVENESS IS A POSTURE, NOT AN ACTION THAT IS EVENT-DRIVEN OR APOLOGY-MOTIVATED.

In Jesus's parable, it is difficult to fathom the attitude of the lender who received the king's forgiveness. After all, his fellow servant was only asking for mercy and patience, not forgiveness. What the lender does next is even more difficult to understand. He throws the debtor into prison *until* he pays! Has he concluded that the debtor won't pay so he might as well be punished? Is his intention to send a message to other debtors? While we don't know his intention, we know the debtor cannot personally pay this debt while imprisoned.

The imprisonment in Jesus's parable correlates to spiritual bondage. When we don't release someone of their offense, we bind them to it—spiritually speaking. While in the prison, they have no way of making it right even if they try. Many people suffer spiritually from being in someone's prison of unforgiveness.

Think of someone who didn't forgive you, even after you tried to make it right. How do you typically feel when in their presence? You likely feel uncomfortable and may act defensively because you are aware that the person can change your disposition at any moment by bringing up your offense. I've seen this in children with unforgiving parents and among unforgiving spouses. These relationships typically revolve around the offender's attempts to keep the other person from getting angry. In this type of predicament, the offender can never seem to satisfy or rectify their offense. The offended person values the offense over the relationship.

When the man in Jesus's parable places his debtor in prison, he feels like he has won. He feels justified in his actions. What he doesn't realize is that he has put himself in the most precarious situation—he has bound himself to a posture of unforgiveness with no way of being free. The offender is now unable to make the situation right. The same is true when we fail to forgive others. What begins as retaliation ends as a posture of unforgiveness that we cannot be released from without the offender's assistance. Essentially, we have bound ourselves to unforgiveness with no way of escape. The spirit of unforgiveness we placed on our debtor is now on us. Over time, this unforgiveness will turn into a spirit of bitterness that will entrench itself deeply in our souls.

Jesus concludes His parable by saying:

> When the other servants saw what had happened, they were outraged and went and told their master everything that had happened. Then the master called the servant in. "You wicked servant," he said, "I canceled all that debt of yours because you begged me to. Shouldn't you have had mercy on your fellow servant just as I had on you?" In anger his master handed him over to the jailers to be tortured, until he should pay back all he owed. This is how my heavenly Father will treat each of you unless you forgive your brother or sister from your heart.
>
> (Matthew 18:31–35)

The actions of the other servants show us what we should do when we see a brother or sister with a perpetual, unrepentant spirit of unforgiveness—go to King Jesus in prayer. In doing so, we inform the King of the injustice and ask Him to deal with it in the manner He sees fit. This is how the kingdom operates. There are times when we know that there is nothing we can do with a fellow servant other than pray. Though we view everyone as redeemable, we know that sometimes, no amount of conversation, counseling, or intervention will do any good. For these types of situations, we have to turn over the unforgiving party to God, so He can handle matters in His own way.

In the parable, when the king finds out about the unforgiving servant's actions, he summons the servant to himself. As Christians, we should never find ourselves in this situation. The forgiveness that we have received from God should lead us to forgive on the spot—immediately and without hesitation. There should be no apology needed, even under the worst of circumstances. We are compelled to forgive because we have been forgiven! We no longer evaluate our brothers and sisters based upon their faults or offenses. Even if we don't deem a particular relationship worth much, we must remember that it is still more important than the offense. In some way or another, every relationship is designed to reveal the level of our maturity in God.

In Jesus's parable, the king calls the unforgiving servant "wicked." This implies that unforgiveness is evil. The king says, "*I canceled all that debt of yours because you begged me to*" (Matthew 18:32). He implies that the forgiveness he showed was not merely a transaction; it should have led to the servant's transformation.

FORGIVENESS SHOULD BE A CATALYST FOR TRANSFORMATION.

When we treat forgiveness as merely a transaction, it serves no larger purpose. It is superficial and shallow at best. Forgiveness should be a catalyst for transformation; we should respond to forgiveness by exhibiting forgiveness to anyone and everyone in need of it.

In Jesus's parable, it seems that the king desires to fill the land with forgiveness. This forgiveness began with him and he expects it to be extended from servant to servant.

Imagine if the forgiven servant had responded to the king by exhibiting the same posture of forgiveness. Instead of reporting his cruelty to the king, his fellow servants would have been musing among themselves about how amazing and wonderful he was for forgiving someone. His generosity would have become contagious throughout the land. It would have become the standard of the kingdom that forgiveness is the best way to deal with an offense.

This kingdom paradigm is missing in the body of Christ today. The spirit of unforgiveness has become a cancer in the church. We have seen it tear apart divinely appointed relationships—anointed leaders and their people, ministries and their destiny, and a myriad of other kingdom agendas—simply because we did not make forgiveness the standard.

But the sad truth is that the forgiven servant in Jesus's parable did not apply the same measure that was given to him. In response, the king does something that only he can do: he reinstates the debt!

With this in mind, we must take forgiveness very seriously. In essence, a true believer doesn't have a choice. Forgiveness is not negotiable; there are no options or justifiable situations that warrant holding a grudge against anyone at any time. The stakes are too high and the ramifications too great to walk in unforgiveness, for even one moment. It's just not worth it!

At the close of His teaching, Jesus says, *"This is how my heavenly Father will treat each of you unless you forgive your brother or sister from your heart"* (Matthew 18:35). For me, this has to be the most important statement for every believer to be conscious of on a daily basis. If this is the measure whereby my membership in the kingdom of heaven is authenticated, then this is something I never want to forget. I need to be reminded daily that forgiveness is not an option. I must forgive because the proof of my transformation depends on it. I can't afford to risk God's anger by holding a grudge in my heart.

7

WE WILL BE OFFENDED

Jesus once said, "It is impossible that no offenses should come, but woe to him through whom they do come!" (Luke 17:1 NKJV). "Offenses" here can also be translated as "causes for stumbling," "stumbling blocks," "things that cause people to stumble," or "temptations," depending on the Bible translation used. Jesus is referring to the reality that some people lead others into sin and how we are to deal with a fellow believer who sins. (See Luke 17:3–4.) Jesus's statement is worrisome to say the least, especially when we spend so much of our time trying to avoid pitfalls.

Jesus's warning indicates that we need to have a sixth sense about our social interactions, so we can see the traps even when they are hidden. Snares are never easily detectable, but they are always there. Within the context of every relationship—whether intimate, casual, distant, or incidental—there is always the potential for an offense because people are flawed and subject to misunderstandings. Often, offenses will be unintentional but look intentional and ill-willed. Most of the time, people do not intend to hurt us.

Unfortunately, we don't approach relationships with the awareness Jesus recommends. We are typically very casual and unsuspecting, even when we are embarking on what could be viewed as an intimate relationship. (Compare 2 Corinthians 6:14–7:1.) Yet nearly every person we meet will cross the threshold of offense at one point or another.

> # NEARLY EVERY PERSON WE MEET WILL CROSS THE THRESHOLD OF OFFENSE AT ONE POINT ANOTHER.

But the more we are able to realize that most people do not intend to harm us, the more we will be able to avoid trapping our relationships in unforgiveness. There is nothing more damaging for any of us than to be emotionally scarred; it can cause us to trap future relationships in the feelings of past relationships. When most people respond to an offense, they are not dealing with the offense itself but an accumulated history of offenses. This entangles every new relationship with old ones, so every new hurt compounds the old hurt.

If snares will be set on my life's journey, and stumbling blocks are inevitable, how should I approach my relationships?

IT'S MORE ABOUT THE OFFENDED THAN THE OFFENDER

Jesus said, *"If your brother or sister sins against you, rebuke them; and if they repent, forgive them. Even if they sin against you seven times in a day and seven times come back to you saying 'I repent,' you must forgive them"* (Luke 17:3–4). Usually, we read these verses from the perspective of self-preservation and thereby miss the powerful meaning of the text. What if the offense—and the situation surrounding it—is more about the offended than the offender? What if the snares of others are only effective because of our outlook? If we look at it this way, everything changes.

It's as if we all walk around with our hurt feelings on our shoulders and we're just waiting for someone to accidently bump into us and knock them off. This makes me think of what my life could have been like—and all of the things I could have avoided—had I realized this. If I had known that my reactions to offenses were the only reason why the snares others set were effective, I could have avoided them all. This is a very uncomfortable feeling because it requires admitting weakness and it requires self-denial. Furthermore, I was never taught this principle in earnest. As a result, the temptation to embrace negative feelings became the bait and the trap of others worked like a charm.

Overcoming this temptation is a life-long quest to some degree. Offenses will come and they are the only way for us to measure our relational growth and maturity. Forgiving when it is difficult—and avoiding falling into relational-based temptations—is essential to becoming qualified for greater responsibility in God's kingdom.

Imagine the calamity for humanity if Jesus had been ensnared by offenses or if He mismanaged His emotions. The harsh words of the Pharisees, the thoughts of the scribes, the fickle nature of the crowds, the outright hatred of the high priests, or the disbelief of his disciples—all could have caused Jesus to stray from His assignment. What a universal catastrophe that would have been! Even in the garden of Gethsemane, the offense of His closest friends—sleeping during some of His most difficult hours—could have distracted Him from His purpose. (See Luke 22:45–46; Matthew 26:40–46.) Yet Jesus maintains His focus; He realizes that His destiny is the cross with or without His friends.

This is why every believer needs to read the Scriptures. Doing so minimizes our issues and highlights the agenda of the kingdom. Jesus was able to deal with every offense, snare, or trap that came His way because He understood that the Father had an agenda that superseded His feelings. The offenses He endured from birth until death paled in comparison to His obligation to fulfill His Father's desire of saving the world from its sins. (See John 3:16–17.)

JESUS UNDERSTOOD THAT THE FATHER HAD AN AGENDA THAT SUPERSEDED HIS FEELINGS.

Imagine if we would revere our assignment the way Jesus did. The little traps and stumbling blocks we deal with wouldn't even be recognized as such because our concerns would be for the things above.

How often do you stumble and fall away from the will and purpose of God due to an offense, snare, or trap that affects your feelings? Do you realize that you may be idolizing your emotions? Why are your feelings treated like hard evidence when they are so temporary and fleeting in nature? I believe the enemy knows that feelings are the most effective way to keep an individual in a constant state of remorse and disarray. On the other hand, how we deal with offenses gives us an opportunity to spiritually mature.

HOW WE SHOULD DEAL WITH OFFENSES

Jesus explains how to deal with those who offend us and sin against us in Luke 17. The context here is similar to the context of Matthew 18. The main differences are that in Luke's account, Jesus's statement is shortened, the two parables are excluded, and the specific questions from the disciples and Peter are omitted. Luke's account also ends in a different parable.

At the outset of Luke's chapter, I am struck by Jesus's directness as He states rather emphatically that offenses (or stumbling blocks) will occur. This puts everyone on alert. We wonder how we will *prepare* for them, *protect* ourselves, and *process* them. If offenses will inevitably come, then we must understand what should be accomplished as a result of them so they are not viewed only from a negative perspective. Jesus's warning is not meant to make us spend our time worrying about the next offense or stumbling block. He warns us so we will not be alarmed when offenses or stumbling blocks come our way. He does not want us to lose our faith or be overcome by them. We need to be able to recover from the experience.

So what must we do in light of this harsh reality? First, we must prepare. We cannot let an offense or stumbling block catch us off-guard. You may not know when it will come, where it will come from, or through whom it will come, but don't be shocked when it comes! The proper preparation will allow you to manage an offense, stumbling block, or temptation, regardless of the source or the season.

PREPARING FOR OFFENSES

Offenses can be challenging because most people are not prepared for them. Whether we are speaking of a personal relationship, an acquaintance, or a situational offense involving a stranger, we are usually ill-equipped to respond in an appropriate fashion.

This keeps us from maturing or developing. A lack of preparation allows offenses to have deep and lasting repercussions. We usually respond inappropriately and allow the conflict to have an extended life. But the proper response could eradicate the long-term effects.

So how do we prepare for an offense? First, we must understand that preparation doesn't mean being guarded. It doesn't mean that we are so protective of ourselves and our emotions that we refuse to open up or be vulnerable. It doesn't mean being unnatural or unapproachable. Instead, preparing for an offense is spiritual; it's about making our inner selves in tune with certain realities.

WE MUST START EACH DAY WITH THE EXPECTATION THAT GOD WANTS TO PERFECT OUR CHARACTER.

I must remind myself that my heavenly Father is sovereign and is ultimately responsible for anything and anyone coming into my life, whether it is interpreted as positive or negative. With a deep sense of God's sovereignty over my affairs, there comes a deep sense of trust. As I develop this trust in the sovereignty of God, it will periodically be tested by way of a person, relationship, or situation. Each time I successfully navigate one of these experiences, I will be able to deepen my trust and confidence in God. I will learn what God is doing and what He expects of me.

What I'm advocating can be more easily understood than experienced. Going through it will definitely be more difficult; in some cases, we will only have understanding in retrospect.

Still, this is the way our Father will perfect this dimension of our development.

We must start each day with the expectation that God wants to perfect our character and we will not adjust on our own. There is a part of me that is rigid, callous, or insensitive that needs to be chiseled away so I will be more useful to the kingdom, so I may be fully equipped to fulfill my destiny. My loving Father will allow for offenses by friend or foe, by stranger or by relative, to help to change me. Thus, my spiritual preparation must include being a worthy and useful vessel. I must have this posture about all of my experiences.

Paul reminds us, *"And we know that in all things God works for the good of those who love him, who have been called according to his purpose"* (Romans 8:28). While we know this to be true, in the midst of a difficulty, the process can feel disconcerting. Therefore, each day, we must use careful discernment about the sovereignty of God.

PROTECTING OURSELVES FROM OFFENSES

We have to *protect* our emotions during an offense. Offenses tend to have such long life because our emotions are deeply involved. We should work to ensure that offenses do not cause permanent emotional damage. Such damage is counterproductive to God's will and plan for our lives. Instead, we should use offenses as an opportunity to be aware of our emotions.

We've all been involved in an argument that went too far, to the point where someone said something they regretted. This was not the plan at the onset of the argument but, with unprotected emotions, the argument got out of control. Most of us have also seen situations escalate to the point of violence and abuse.

Genesis provides us with an example of a regrettable reaction: Cain's actions against God and his brother Abel. (See Genesis 4:1–16.) Cain and Abel are given the same opportunity to worship YHWH. Cain offered Him *"some of the fruits of the soil,"* whereas Abel offered *"fat portions from some of the firstborn of his flock"* (Genesis 4:3–4). God accepts Abel's offering, but Cain's is rejected. Cain, being the older brother, is embarrassed, upset, and offended by this rejection. He then becomes emotional. God sees and acknowledges his emotions and gives him instruction, offering him an opportunity to make things right. (See Genesis 4:6–7.) Instead of taking inventory of his actions to determine why YHWH did not accept his offering, Cain choses to allow his emotions to dictate his response, even after being warned of the consequences. This is an example of how unprotected emotions can drive us away from God's plan.

UNPROTECTED EMOTIONS CAN DRIVE US AWAY FROM GOD'S PLAN.

When God approaches Cain, He obviously wants him to comprehend his error and his emotional state and make the necessary adjustments so he can move on and be successful in his worship. Cain is given the same opportunity we are all given: take inventory and try again. God asks him, *"Why are you angry? Why is your face downcast?"* (Genesis 4:6). Both of these questions address Cain's emotional state. It is up to Cain to decide how he will respond.

The rest of the story shows us how Cain did not heed the counsel of God but instead allowed his emotions to rule over him and carry him into sin. Cain's anger evolves into the regrettable and tragic premeditated murder of his own brother.

In Cain's case, a perceived offense developed into anger, which then evolved into hatred and then into murder. Cain justifies murder based on his emotions. Have you seen this type of emotional pattern in your own life? At the end of the offense equation, we simply walk away from a regrettable and avoidable result, feeling justified because of our emotional state. Chances are no one has ever challenged you to repent. So here we are, many of us in the same predicament as Cain, not realizing that we too can end up as fugitives and vagabonds, never regaining the strength to truly deal with our emotional state.

We must protect our emotions before they control us.

PROCESSING OFFENSES

We know that preparing for offenses requires an acute awareness of God's purpose for our lives. But how should we *process* offenses?

It has been said that the most primary instinct of human nature is self-preservation. This is why it is so difficult to deal with offenses. We are so devoted to protecting ourselves that we very seldom allow ourselves to become vulnerable. But vulnerability allows us to process offenses.

This is well-illustrated by the experience of commercial airline pilots. For the duration of their careers, these pilots must periodically go through training and retraining to ensure they are current with new technologies and certifications. A portion of their training is committed to preparing for and processing unforeseen circumstances. During this training, the pilots enter a simulator to practice handling emergencies. They are made vulnerable and are challenged to process the events they are put through. Their job is to preserve life and the integrity of the aircraft to the best of their abilities. They are trained to keep their emotions at bay while in a state of emergency.

Pilots don't take emergencies personally and they don't get emotional. They are trained to be ready for the unexpected with the desire to correct, compensate, and calculate for a positive outcome. They then debrief after the event to better understand how they and other pilots can handle similar events in the future. They welcome the process.

We hold a pilot to high standards because of the responsibility involved in flying an aircraft filled with people, yet we place few standards on our emotional health.

Unlike pilots, most people don't take the time to process situations, either because they are too preoccupied with self-preservation or they are only concerned with how they feel. Generally, when people feel emotionally justified in what they do, that's all that matters to them. When we function like this, we are ill-equipped to process offenses and grow. We are ill-equipped for the work of the kingdom.

Like a pilot during an emergency, we should process what's happening during an offense, so we can better identify what emotions may be triggered and thereby manage them. We need to learn to make better decisions and have better responses to the situations that present themselves. This is easier said than done, but with practice, we can grow. When we become more aware of our knee-jerk reactions to the unexpected, we can temper them. This process requires self-control, which is rarely acquired without deep introspection or training.

THE INEVITABILITY OF OFFENSES

As Jesus taught us, we must accept that offenses will come—typically without warning. They will catch you off guard when you are feeling good about yourself, your circumstances, or life in general. They will interrupt a good day. They will show up when you are tired or distracted. They will disrupt the peace. They will rain on your parade. They will interrupt your perfect plans. Offenses will come at the wrong time and will challenge you to the core. It is at this point that the discipline of self-control—and the habit of processing before responding—will be your only friend.

OFFENSES WILL CATCH YOU OFF GUARD AND CHALLENGE YOU TO THE CORE.

When these habits are effectively applied to your life, you will find yourself identifying the particular emotions that trigger negative reactions. You can then learn to manage these emotions before they dominate and dictate your response. This is the goal. Once this is accomplished, offenses can serve a positive purpose in our lives. Like an airline pilot, we can begin to welcome offenses because they will assist us in acquiring new skills and knowledge. They will teach us how to handle future unforeseen circumstances.

Joseph's life was plagued with people who repeatedly offended him. (See Genesis 37–50.) It begins with his immediate family—who typically provide us with the most difficult offenses to handle—and continues all the way to the wife of his boss. What Joseph endures would devastate the best of us. Yet Joseph is somehow able to handle each painful word and action that come his way.

When you read his story in the book of Genesis, Joseph does not seem to be overly spiritual or especially godly. At best, we can presume that his dreams kept him grounded in his belief system and his belief system caused him to regard everything as a part of God's process for his life. We have nothing else to extract from his life to explain his endurance. Joseph's dreams serve as a parallel to our kingdom responsibility and the need for a kingdom perspective.

The reality of our dream, vision, or purpose—God's work in us—is the reason why we have to be tested with offenses throughout our lives. We are not suited to do what God has designed for us until our temperament has been tested, tried, and proved. This process may not be what we would expect, but in my view, it is what God has prescribed. And for Joseph, this led him all the way to becoming the manager of the nation of Egypt.

We generally think that our best opportunity to become a CEO is to attend a notable business school, have a great internship, and then network with the right people in our field of choice. But in Joseph's case, apparently, the best training and testing to see if he could manage the nation of Egypt was to have his brothers, friends, and associates wrong him. Joseph's story shows that offenses are the only true test of character and spiritual maturity.

Joseph's brothers plot to kill him and then sell him into slavery. (See Genesis 37.) The wife of his boss fabricates a story about him, but rather than being ensnared in anger, Joseph carries himself with integrity and dignity. (See Genesis 39.) He was careful not to put himself in a compromising position—exhibiting exemplary character—yet a scandal broke out against him. I don't think we can comprehend the emotional and psychological impact this kind of scandal would bring on a normal person. But Joseph somehow became stronger.

These kinds of difficulties prepare us and test us, so that, like Joseph, our dreams may become our real lives. This goes against everything we have been taught and trained to accept.

Most people respond to difficulties in a way contrary to Joseph's. Our self-preservation instincts kick in and we retaliate.

We put up a line of defense to intimidate the next possible offender. We become experts at letting people know what we will not tolerate, under any circumstances. Our personal billboards clearly state, "You cross this line and I will cut your head off!" Turning the other cheek is the last thing on our minds when slapped by some insensitive idiot.

Yet these moments of difficulty and scandal reveal everything about our readiness to move to the next level of what God has planned for us. The scandal gauges our level of humility. And humility is a prerequisite for our elevation.

Often, when difficulty comes along, we bow out of the process and rest in our accomplishments. We are so content with our accomplishments that we forfeit the next level of influence God has planned for us; we assume that success was the thing to strive for. If we would only begin to reinterpret the purpose of difficulties, we would begin to see the glory of God revealed in our lives in a whole new way. It's not about bringing you down; it's really about raising you up.

Once we understand how God can use offenses, we can begin to respond to people in a totally different way. Instead of focusing on the offense and the offender, it can shift to, "How do I protect my emotions during this process and emerge better for having gone through it?"

Ultimately, we know that life would be different by the simple application of these steps during an offense. We would be different emotionally, spiritually, and psychologically. Most of all, we would be better equipped to handle the unexpected problems and dilemmas of life.

Imagine if your past relationships were approached with this mindset. How many relationships would have been spared grief and sorrow? How many relationships could have avoided catastrophe? How might our hearts have been spared from extreme disappointment? How might we have looked beyond the fault and saw the need?

THE BALANCE OF JESUS'S WORDS ABOUT OFFENSES

Let's consider again what Jesus said about offenses: *"It is impossible that no offenses should come, but woe to him through whom they do come!"* (Luke 17:1 NKJV). This is a point of introspection. We don't want to be the offender. Jesus severely judges the one who offends or attempts to cause another to stumble, even though the offense may serve a larger purpose.

JESUS SEVERELY JUDGES THE ONE WHO OFFENDS OR ATTEMPTS TO CAUSE ANOTHER TO STUMBLE.

Those who offend, or cause others to stumble, are typically acting out of selfish or insensitive motivations. We cannot claim to be brilliant enough to design an offense that could serve the advancement of the Lord's purpose in someone's life. Furthermore, Jesus is not talking about your typical mistake or act of insensitivity. He is talking about an action that causes someone to fall away from their walk of faith and return to sinning. This entrapment is what is so offensive to Jesus and warrants His dramatic judgment.

Jesus goes so far as to say it would be better for the offender to die than to lead another astray. (See Luke 17:2.) This declaration makes me wonder if we have any idea how seriously the Father takes the act of ensnaring one of His children. Though it may look like the offense is against an individual, it's actually against the Lord. That is why the ramifications are so serious.

If we take the time to view our potential offenses to others in this light, how cautious would we be before we acted? Jesus is announcing a death warrant for offenses that cause people to fall away from the faith.

And lest we think we don't make these kinds of mistakes, let's remember how many people leave the church due to an offense and never return again. Furthermore, our church leaders are being called to task here because they are often responsible for the actions and reactions of people in the congregation. We cannot overlook the fact that believers are precious to God. Thus, leaders will be held accountable for their part in discouraging Christians. (See James 3:1.)

Personally, I've experienced discouragement and offenses in several churches. I must say, if I were not mature in my own walk, those offenses would have caused me to depart from the faith and never return. Church environments can be so callous and egotistical that even leaders turn on other leaders and cause them to stumble. This being the case among leaders, you know the members will be subject to even greater harm. So being a leader myself and knowing the pain of "church hurt," I want to do my part in providing an opportunity for those who have been hurt and abused by the church. I want to do my part to lead with integrity.

Jesus says, *"Take heed to yourselves"* (Luke 17:3 NKJV). We are the only ones who can stop this perpetuation of wrongdoing. Take the time to think about your words before you release them. Think about the motivation behind those words. Think about the impact of those words in the short-term and long-term. Examine how you would feel if the same words were spoken to you. Think about alternative ways to deliver a message. Consider not responding at all as a first alternative, instead of a last alternative. Pray before you speak. Laugh it off. Ignore it. Absorb it. Be mature. Be an example. Whatever you do, don't just react—respond. Remember that what you say or do may be a snare for your brother or sister and thus be an offense to God!

From sunrise to sunrise, life is full of offenses. Walk in a posture of forgiveness as a way of life and these offenses will have less of an impact on you. Although snares will be set along your way, you will have a greater ability to slip right out of them, even when they seem to have been perfectly set. Forgiveness is the key that unlocks the snare.

THINGS SIMPLY DON'T GO ACCORDING TO PLAN

At a certain point in life, we all begin to realize that things don't always go according to plan. We all part with our idealism at some juncture and live with the reality of unpredictability. We each must participate in the unpredictable plan of God, which includes twists and turns, bumps and bruises, nicks and cuts, and the eventual knowledge of His will. As we become more acquainted with this process, we become less frustrated by the things that happen to us and more confident in the sovereignty of our God.

We must learn to welcome offenses. We must learn to become comfortable with interruptions.

Prepare each and every day for experiences that will develop you. Be *protective* of your emotional state and be aware of your emotional triggers so you can manage your responses better. And finally, *process* these incidents in such a way that it improves your character and maintains your relationships.

We must remember Jesus's words, *"Truly I tell you, unless you change and become like little children, you will never enter the kingdom of heaven"* (Matthew 18:3). We associate little children with a lot of characteristics and qualities to help us understand what Jesus is saying. However, we don't usually acknowledge that one of the experiences of childhood is being offended so we may grow and mature.

I remember vividly how my parents offended me (on the cushiony part of my anatomy) on a regular basis. There were times after those offenses that I said to myself, in my immaturity, "I'm not going to kiss them goodnight or say 'I love you.'" I was so offended by the spanking that I was willing to emotionally discard the relationship. But it didn't take long for me to mature and process what they were trying to teach me. I would eventually realize that I was wrong. I considered that they provided for my well-being and discarding the relationship would have worse repercussions for me than for them. Also, I could see that their form of discipline, though unpleasant, was not designed to destroy me but to change me for the better.

OFFENSES CAN BECOME THE MOST POWERFUL OPPORTUNITY FOR YOU DEVELOP AS A PERSON.

When Jesus says we must become like children, we must also consider the process whereby a child matures and develops. This process often includes offenses.

I hope that offenses will now take on a different meaning in your life. They can become the most powerful opportunity for you develop as a person. Remember that you have a mandate from the Father on your life. He wants to do something through you that is designed expressly for you. It will only be accomplished after you fulfill certain maturity requirements. The quicker you mature, the faster you will achieve those mandates.

As Jesus was preparing for His departure, He told His disciples that He had much more to share with them, but they could not yet handle it. (See John 16:12.) Part of the disciples' ability to handle the new information would be directly related to their maturity, which would come through the presence of the Holy Spirit and their difficult experiences.

At this point, I'm sure you are reevaluating some of the offenses of your past and trying to ascertain their significance, especially as they relate to how God will accomplish His purposes in your life. You should be seeing the opportunities you missed or the ones you need to revisit. You may be seeing how God's elevation of your life has been delayed or stopped because you were more concerned with self-preservation than spiritual development and maturity. Maybe now the picture is becoming clear for you and you are beginning to see how you can get out of the quagmire that unforgiveness creates.

If this is the case, take a moment now to put this book aside and allow the Lord to clear every emotional and spiritual hindrance out of your mind and spirit, so you can release the glory of the Lord on your life in this very moment.

After all, what good would these words really be if they were not applied? The reality is that no one who reads this book is exempt. Jesus's statements apply to everyone and everyone has to respond to Him.

LIVING WITH A POSTURE OF FORGIVENESS REQUIRES MENTAL AND EMOTIONAL DISCIPLINE.

The practice of handling offenses in a new way won't be easy at first. Mental and emotional discipline is imperative. Each test will dig deeper into your psyche and will require a deeper commitment. You must remember that even when you think you've got it, something will come out of left field. The key is to remain focused on your purpose, dream, or vision, and give less liberty to your emotions. This will ensure your success.

As you contemplate your desire to be a vessel suited for the kingdom, prepare yourself for offenses. Welcome them as a necessary part of your growth process.

PART THREE:

FORGIVENESS IS THE KEY TO HEALING AND RELATIONSHIPS

8

HEALING STARTS
WITH FORGIVENESS

The knowledge that people will inevitably offend us (see Luke 17:1) helps to keep us centered and grounded, but it still may not be enough to motivate us to forgive. For that, we need a major reorientation. After all, our mental and emotional defense mechanisms are very strong. We need to shift into a new posture of forgiveness. This is why Jesus emphasizes that the real motivation to forgive is our Father's response to an unforgiving spirit.

THE FATHER TREATS US AS WE TREAT OTHERS

When it comes to forgiveness, Jesus says our heavenly Father will treat us in the same way we treat others. (See Matthew 18:35.) This is the ultimate motivation to have a spirit of forgiveness. This often-ignored New Testament concept is introduced by Jesus to radically shift us into a posture of forgiveness. If we understand that forgiveness has nothing to do with measuring and contemplating the greatness of the offense, then we can act more swiftly and forgive more readily. Jesus essentially says that if you desire to receive the full benefits of being forgiven by the Father—which is ultimately the desire and expectation of every believer—then you must forgive without conditions.

Jesus illustrates this point again in the Disciples' Prayer, also called the Lord's Prayer: *"Forgive us our debts, as we also have forgiven our debtors"* (Matthew 6:12). The removal of our debts demands that we forgive the debts of others. Jesus could even be implying that if we don't forgive the debts of others, our debts will not be forgiven. The first part of this verse is often translated, *"Forgive us our **trespasses**,"* but *"Forgive us our **debts**"* is a more literal reading.

Jesus then emphasizes this point. Of all of the things Jesus could have reiterated after the prayer, He goes back to the forgiveness verses and reemphasizes them with further elaboration:

> For if you forgive men their trespasses, your heavenly Father will also forgive you. But if you do not forgive men their trespasses, neither will your Father forgive your trespasses.
>
> (Matthew 6:14–15 NKJV)

This can be read as creating a contingency for our forgiveness by our heavenly Father; at the very least, Jesus is saying we are obligated to forgive.

To fully understand Matthew 6:14–15, we need to look back to Matthew 6:12. Why does Jesus use debt terminology when He could have easily said, "Forgive us for our wrongs as we forgive those who have wronged us"? This could have accomplished the same goal of encouraging the disciples to forgive. However, Jesus doesn't want to encourage His listeners to merely forgive; He wants them to understand they are under an inflexible obligation to forgive. There is no option for disciples of Jesus. They owe it to God to forgive.

Jesus's language shifts our perspective of forgiveness away from the type or level of an offense to the degree of obedience we owe the Father because of how much He has forgiven us. This changes the equation of forgiveness completely. From this vantage point, the degree of offense is never the measure for whether or not someone is worthy of forgiveness. The measure is always directly related to how obedient I am as a disciple of Jesus.

THE DISCIPLES OF JESUS OWE IT TO GOD TO FORGIVE.

The end of the Lord's Prayer in Luke's gospel is slightly different than Matthew's version. It reads, *"And forgive us our sins, for we also forgive everyone who is indebted to us"* (Luke 11:4 NKJV). Our sin is a debt to God that is impossible to pay; the very knowledge of it should make it easy to forgive those who are indebted to us.

To fully understand the theology here, we need to go back to Matthew's gospel. At the Last Supper, Jesus says, *"This is my blood of the covenant, which is poured out for many for the forgiveness of sins"* (Matthew 26:28). Because of Jesus, God the Father has pardoned and freed us from our insurmountable debt without asking us to participate, even remotely, in the payment process.

Forgiveness, then, is how we distinguish the merely religious from those who are truly in a relationship with the Father through Jesus Christ. To make this distinction clear, in the preamble to the Disciples' Prayer, Jesus highlights how the hypocrites pray. (See Matthew 6:5–8.) I'm sure that in Jesus's day, as in our time, many people felt inadequate when they heard the eloquent prayers of the lofty. In response, Jesus says the authenticity of prayer can best be measured by the way a person forgives others. If a person is incapable of managing forgiveness on earth, then it is highly unlikely that God is even reacting to the prayers that have elevated them in the people's eyes.

The best way, and possibly the only way, to exhibit the evidence of your sins being forgiven—and thus authenticate your relationship with the Father—is to forgive others. There should be no struggle, no amount of pride, and no apology needed. Nor should the level of offense keep you from immediately forgiving others. With God, there was no struggle, pride, lack of an apology, or level of offense that kept Him from appointing His Son—before the foundations of the world—to suffer, die, and rise for the forgiveness our sins. A hallelujah should be said right here!

A WITHERED FIG TREE AND THE POWER OF FAITH

The gospel of Mark puts another fascinating twist on the theology of forgiveness. Jesus rebukes a fig tree because it has no figs for Him when He's hungry. (See Mark 11:12–14.) Later, when He and his disciples pass it again, Peter notices the tree is dried up from the roots, which suggests it had toppled over and the roots were visible, thus rendering the tree dead. (See Mark 11:20–26.) Peter marvels at the fact that this is the same tree Jesus recently spoke to and cursed. This remark brings an immediate and succinct imperative from Jesus: *"Have faith in God"* (Mark 11:22).

But why does Jesus respond this way? The surrounding context offers some clues.

First, Jesus had experienced an overly exuberant crowd of well-wishers when He entered Jerusalem. (See Mark 11:1–11.) The response of these people will prove to be fleeting; by the end of the week, Jesus is arrested, tried, and crucified. He has also recently driven all the merchandisers out from the Jerusalem Temple, highlighting the hypocrisy of the whole religious experience in the city. (See Mark 11:15–19.) In between these two moments, Jesus sees a fig tree full of leaves but no figs. He is so disappointed, He tells the tree, *"May no one ever eat fruit from you again"* (Mark 11:14).

If we follow the story in its entirety, we know Jesus is about to die at the hands of the religious establishment. If you knew you were about to be killed by the very people you came to restore and redeem, this would undoubtedly have an adverse effect on your psyche. You might even react negatively to those who are with you, fully aware that they will abandon you.

In this regard, it seems Jesus spoke to the tree out of His frustration with the season of life He was in. Jesus wishes the tree would bear fruit—and likewise wishes the same for the people of Jerusalem. The power and authority that Jesus speaks with causes the tree to be recognizably lifeless right away.

I can almost hear Peter's voice, with wild amazement and exuberance, as he proclaims, *"Rabbi, look! The fig tree you cursed has withered"* (Mark 11:21). The unspoken question behind Peter's statement is, "Can we also do this?" There is no doubt that such an unusual and immediate manifestation warranted some type of explanation. Thanks to Peter's outburst, the explanation comes immediately, but is not immediately understood.

WE NEED TO UNDERSTAND THAT GOD HIMSELF HAS FAITH.

Jesus tells Peter, *"Have faith in God"* (Mark 11:22). What does this mean and what does it have to do with the dead fig tree? The answer starts with the application of a more practical understanding of faith. Jesus is not referring to hoping, wishing, or believing without a corresponding action. Faith is, in many ways, practical and perceivable. This is the faith the disciples will need in order to perpetuate the kingdom upon Jesus's departure. This faith will get the same results that Jesus got and will cause the disciples to see greater works in His absence. (See John 14:12–14.)

But how does this faith look different than what we practice?

Understanding the faith Jesus is advocating starts with the basic yet profound understanding that God Himself has faith! The writer of the book of Hebrews explains this in the opening verses of chapter eleven, often called the "hall of faith."

> *Now faith is the substance of things hoped for, the evidence of things not seen. For by it the elders obtained a good testimony. By faith we understand that the worlds were framed by the word of God, so that the things which are seen were not made of things which are visible.* (Hebrews 11:1–3 NKJV)

Faith is the substance and evidence of things that are expected, but not yet revealed in the natural realm. By having faith, our spiritual elders—the believers of the past—gained a good report from God. *"By faith...the worlds were framed by the word of God."* Since I know that God framed the world with His words, God is the first in a long list of faithful elders. Before the elders, God set an example; God achieved forming the world by His faith.

In Genesis 1:3, *"God said, 'Let there be light,' and there was light."* But it was not until day four that He created the sun, moon, and stars. (See Genesis 1:14–19.) Yet when God *said* let there be light, *there was light.* The substance of God's faith is in His words—when God spoke, His faith was immediately manifested in light, even before the mechanisms of light were present.

In the same manner, Jesus explains to Peter that he too can curse and whither a fig tree—if he has faith. Jesus's faith made the tree dead upon speaking the words; the result, like the source of light, was manifest later. Jesus backs His declaration by teaching His disciples the practical process whereby they will get the same results He did:

*For assuredly, I say to you, whoever says to this mountain,
"Be removed and be cast into the sea," and does not doubt in
his heart, but believes that those things he says will be done, he
will have whatever he says. Therefore I say to you, whatever
things you ask when you pray, believe that you receive them,
and you will have them. And whenever you stand praying,
if you have anything against anyone, forgive him, that your
Father in heaven may also forgive you your trespasses. But if
you do not forgive, neither will your Father in heaven forgive
your trespasses.* (Mark 11:23–26 NKJV)

Jesus says belief and spoken words—with the absence of
doubt—will bring what we declare. This means you cannot merely
believe; you have to say something! *Saying something* is the substance and evidence of our belief that brings about the visible
result. Just as God spoke at creation, so must we speak. If there
are no words corresponding to the internal belief, there will not be
any visible result.

In Mark 11:24, Jesus repeats the same declaration, but He
changes it slightly, from just saying something to *praying* something. This shifts the context to include our heavenly Father in the
process. Now we are praying something to the Father and He will
ensure that our prayers are answered. This subtle but very important shift causes us to look beyond ourselves to our walk of faith
with the Father. If He is to be included in the equation, then I
must be on speaking terms with Him and He must be able to hear
and respond to my prayer.

This is where we shift back to the value and importance of
forgiveness.

The manifestation of your words and prayers are representative of an authentic relationship with the Father that is confirmed
by communication based upon honesty. The honesty is based upon
the reality of my fault and the certainty of God's forgiveness. My

communication with the Father would not exist without the reality of His forgiveness. Every time I communicate to the Father about anything, I do it knowing the only reason I have this privilege is because He has already forgiven me. In essence, forgiveness is the basis upon which I receive any miracle from my Father.

FORGIVENESS IS THE BASIS UPON WHICH I RECEIVE ANY MIRACLE FROM MY FATHER.

For me, when reading Mark 11:22–26, I used to disconnect the last two verses, viewing them in a separate context, because many English Bibles break this discourse into two paragraphs. However, the subject matter does not shift—instead, it is a continuation of Jesus's teaching on faith and prayer. Thus, for Jesus, the request for miracles and forgiveness are interconnected.

Jesus seems to be indicating that miraculous manifestations are not available to those who are not forgiving others. The unforgiving tongue is not capable of getting a miraculous response from heaven because there is an obstruction between it and the Father. Here, Jesus again confirms that we must forgive as we have been forgiven. This powerful concept is central to our prayers for miracles.

THE RELATIONSHIP BETWEEN FORGIVENESS AND MIRACLES

When Jesus got the miraculous result with the fig tree, it amazed Peter not just because of the immediacy of the manifestation, but also because it was proof that Jesus truly had an uninterrupted relationship with the Father. Nowadays, we have a lot of people saying they have a relationship with God, but very few of us have supernatural evidence of that relationship. Forgiveness stands in our way. In contrast, Jesus certainly had good reasons to be unforgiving and hold a grudge, yet He remained completely forgiving. This enabled Him to speak with the authority of heaven on His side and receive the results He desired.

To emulate Jesus, we need to use our tongue in a consistent fashion. (See James 1:26.) This consistency is critical to our ability to speak authoritatively, both when we forgive and when we move mountains with our faith. (See Mark 11:23–26.) Both actions are representative of our relationship with the Father.

They are also related in another way. For many of us, the act of forgiving someone who has willfully wronged us is like moving a big mountain. We focus on the offense and how it affected us until it gets bigger in our mind than it actually is. We exacerbate it, embellish it, and expand it to the point that it becomes an immoveable mountain to us. Then we expect the person who offended us to apologize in a magnanimous way to appease the new and exaggerated size of the offense in our minds. But if the offender minimizes what they did, we become furious and tighten our grip on the offense. By the time we are truly able to deal with the offense, we are the ones in need of deliverance, not the offender.

It is amazing how the enemy plays the game of deceiving us so effectively. If our understanding and theology of forgiveness were different, he would have far less power.

TO MAINTAIN AN UNINTERRUPTED CONNECTION WITH THE FATHER, WE MUST FORGIVE IMMEDIATELY.

To maintain an uninterrupted connection with the Father, we must forgive immediately, without any consideration of the level of offense, the person who committed the offense, or whether they apologize. In this way, we exemplify the relationship that we enjoy with the Father and thus enjoy the luxury of walking in His power and authority.

We must remember the example of Jesus. If anyone could have rightly struggled with forgiveness, it would have been the innocent one, Jesus, toward the guilty. Yet He continually forgave. And this brings up part of the problem with human forgiveness: somewhere in the hidden recesses of our mind, we view ourselves as innocent. In particular situations, we are not guilty of being the offender—but this does not make us innocent. Innocence is only applicable if we have never offended anyone and only Jesus can truly claim that posture. Thus, we must be continually forgiving. If we desire to see God manifest miracles through us, the story of the fig tree—and Jesus's subsequent teaching—suggests that forgiveness is a necessity.

In connecting forgiveness and miracles, our heavenly Father was ingenious. He knew that otherwise, we would be biased and condition our miracles upon others apologizing or paying their debts.

We must also remember that only the Holy Spirit can truly convict a person's heart enough for them to change. If we are manipulating a person into remorse, they are not expressing true conviction. If we really value our connection to our heavenly Father, then we will forgive aside from the other person's conviction. (See Mark 11:25–26.) After all, Jesus said we can be forgiven of all sins except one:

> Truly I tell you, people can be forgiven all their sins and every slander they utter, but whoever blasphemes against the Holy Spirit will never be forgiven; they are guilty of an eternal sin.
>
> (Mark 3:28–29)

Since God is able to remove all other offenses from us, how could we possibly hold an offense against our brother or sister? Our worst hurt is still not comparable to God's hurt. Furthermore, our divine connection is worth much more than holding unforgiveness in our heart for even a moment.

While the reality of the interconnection between forgiveness and our relationship to the Father does not make forgiving any easier, it does emphasize the need to forgive. Furthermore, the spirit and psychology of immediate forgiveness can be practiced to the point where it feels natural, to the point where it becomes the most important part of our spiritual walk. We must regularly tell ourselves, with conviction:

> As long as I'm alive, I will need forgiveness and therefore I will need to forgive. In any relationship I enter into, I must enter it prepared to forgive, knowing that at some point, this preparation will be fully employed.

Forgiveness must be more real than our church participation, our shouting and dancing, our speaking in other tongues, our signs and wonders, or our titles and occupations. It has to be the defining characteristic of our Christian posture.

9

CHANGING THE PARADIGM OF FORGIVENESS

Give, and it will be given to you. A good measure, pressed down, shaken together and running over, will be poured into your lap. For with the measure you use, it will be measured to you. (Luke 6:38)

This verse is traditionally used to inspire people to give money at offering time in churches. Though it can be applied that way, the context of the verse suggests it is primarily about how you to treat others. The prior verse shows this to be the case: *"Do not judge, and you will not be judged. Do not condemn, and you will not be condemned. Forgive, and you will be forgiven"* (Luke 6:37). In this context, the giving and receiving in the next verse is about our relationships. It is a transaction that takes place continually and repeatedly throughout our lives. Thus, although we can apply Luke 6:38 to money, it should also be applied to love, judgment, condemnation, mercy, and, above all else, to forgiveness. A kingdom principle is at work here and it is critical to how the kingdom operates overall.

If you give forgiveness, you will receive forgiveness in abundance. However, the process is not initiated by the other person's apology. It is initiated by the willingness to forgive. Herein lies the difficulty for most people. Since the context of forgiveness in our society has been based on a heartfelt, well-rehearsed, sincere, and believable apology, we usually miss the opportunity to give and then receive.

The act of forgiveness—viewed from its most pure perspective and definition—involves the removal of an offense altogether. Every time we forgive, we take it upon ourselves to eradicate a real and true offense and act as if it never happened. This is the part about forgiveness that is a struggle for most people. True forgiveness is emotionally very difficult.

THE BIGGEST DILEMMA OF FORGIVENESS IS THAT GOD IS REQUIRING COURAGE FROM THE PERSON WHO HAS BEEN OFFENDED.

True forgiveness makes it seem like the offender has gotten away with the offense, without paying the "proper penalty." The offended has been inflicted with pain while the offender walks away without a scratch. It's like the scales of justice are imbalanced. Why would a *just* God require such an act of courage from the person who has been offended and not the other way around? This is indeed the biggest dilemma of forgiveness.

THE PARADIGM OF THE OFFENDED

To understand the meaning of godly forgiveness, we must reconsider the paradigm of the offended, based upon God's expectation and requirement of us when we've been hurt. This reconsideration starts with the question, "Why am I offended?" This is almost never considered as a part of the forgiveness process when the offense is deep, blatant, demoralizing, or devastating.

After spending some time dwelling on a minor error or offense, a person may ask, "Why am I offended?" Such scenarios usually lead to the offended person saying, "I will let it go." However, in the case of a deep and devastating offense, that same posture is harder to assume. But I believe God is requiring the same attitude and response of us, regardless of the level of the offense or the repetitive habit of the offender.

God has forgiven us for sins beyond measure. From His perspective, we should forgive quickly and regularly. Thus, you should never enter into a close relationship with anyone who you are not fully prepared to forgive, even for the most hideous offense. I know this is a lot to ask, but ultimately, it is necessary. If you don't feel like you are capable of that kind of forgiveness, it would be best to keep your relationship with that person gracious yet casual.

People are imperfect. Each person's imperfections will surface over time and inevitably offend you in some way, just as your imperfections will offend them. Since we already know this, we should not ignore this reality. We must train our mind, emotions, and spirit to be less offended, and forgive more easily. This seems to be the underlying expectation of Jesus's teaching in chapter six of Luke's gospel, since He is requiring us to forgive like Him without even receiving an apology. (Compare Luke 23:34.) If we cannot forgive like this, it will be virtually impossible for many of us to be released from the pain of the offense.

For these reasons, I have come to the conclusion that part of the forgiveness equation is not being offended so easily. Eventually, our goal should be to not take offense at all. In this way, you can manage difficult situations without the weighty emotional baggage.

Now let me be the first to say that writing this and practicing this are two completely different things. The reality is it may not even be entirely possible to accomplish this in the flesh due to our emotional makeup. However, this does not exempt us from the subtle implication of the Scriptures. If we are obligated to forgive, we should also strive to be less affected by offenses over time.

Certainly I have to admit that in life, there are people who offend you on purpose with the desire to inflict pain. There are those who don't have your best interests at heart. There are those who are seemingly sent as a thorn in your flesh to antagonize you and cause you to stumble. Yet in each of these most unimaginable circumstances, the offended is required to "give" forgiveness. This giving of forgiveness lines up with the perspective that we give as a principle of life in the kingdom. We willingly apply the principle of the *"good measure"* to monetary offerings, but seldom apply it to the act of forgiveness, even though forgiveness is the original context. (See Luke 6:37–38.)

THE PARADIGM OF THE DIVINE PERSPECTIVE

We may be asking ourselves, *Why would God require the offended to give forgiveness without an apology?* To understand this, we must look at forgiveness from the divine perspective.

As YHWH was prepared to deal with Adam's offense before He even made Adam, so we are now invited and encouraged to tap into our divine capacity by doing the same. Now some might say this is really asking too much from a mere human. But I must remind you that you were created in God's image and thus you have His capacity for forgiveness. (See Genesis 1:26–27.) Not only do we have the capacity to forgive in our very nature, but we also need to experience a divine level of power over all of our emotions. This is the catalyst for us being more like God in general.

God's task of forgiveness was much greater than ours. Before he sinned, Adam was perfect and had no history of offense. If it were possible, God would have been surprised and extremely offended that His perfect creation disappointed Him at such a high level. Yet God was totally prepared to remove the offense and apply it to the innocent animal that was killed in Adam's stead. (See Genesis 3:21.) This was an extraordinary display of true forgiveness extended without Adam even apologizing.

Is God expecting us to act as people with the divine spark, in the midst of our humanity? Yes. He is saying that in the most challenging and emotionally charged circumstances, you have the capacity and the ability to be like Him. Living in God's image is not just about praying, loving one another, and sharing our spiritual gifts; it's about forgiving the way He forgives. You will have to forgive over and over, day in and day out, periodically and continually, for the rest of your life. Being able to forgive like God is perhaps the most divine thing you can do.

BEING ABLE TO FORGIVE LIKE GOD IS PERHAPS THE MOST DIVINE THING YOU CAN DO.

The "why" of the forgiveness equation is because God did it with Adam. God forgave and He is the only one who has the right *not* to forgive because He is perfect and without offense. God chose to forgive when Adam and Eve were hiding instead of confessing. (See Genesis 3:10.) He chose to forgive when they were passing the blame. (See Genesis 3:12–13.) He chose to forgive when there was no apparent apology involved. He chose to forgive when they had no real excuse for their actions. He just *chose* to forgive.

Meanwhile, here we are offended, hurt, disappointed, demoralized, devastated—you name it, we feel it. And we are being told that we must give forgiveness. This can only happen when the kingdom principle of giving is taken to another level, when we say to ourselves, "I want to receive what I have given in good measure, shaken together and running over!"

We must be able to say the following, as part of our daily devotions:

> I want to be forgiven by others in the same way that I forgive. I am aware of my imperfections and my ability to offend, just as I have been offended.
>
> I practice giving forgiveness because my offenses toward my God are more numerous than I am able to count and more continual than I care to admit.
>
> Knowing that I offend God and don't apologize for days, weeks, years, and in many cases ever, I would like to be the beneficiary of ultimate forgiveness. Knowing that God is perfect and has never offended anyone, I desire for Him to not hold my imperfections against me.
>
> I trust that God remembers my makeup and knows that I am but dust.
>
> My attitude toward my offender is influenced by the attitude of God and the kingdom that I am a part of.
>
> My attitude is motivated by the kingdom principle of giving forgiveness. My attitude has everything to do with the way I want to be treated, whether in a slight error or a grave offense.
>
> My attitude says that the love of Christ is visible in me in the way I respond to repeated offenses. My attitude says

it is more valuable for me to be forgiven by my heavenly Father than anything else in the world.

Therefore, I make myself less able to take offense so it will be easier to keep the covenant relationship fresh with my Lord. This is the true sign of my kingdom affiliation.

Religion has given us a bunch of false measures whereby we feel secure in our faith. We have used our services, offerings, positions, accomplishments, titles, and more to make ourselves feel spiritually secure. We have left forgiveness as a non-qualifier. However, the ability to forgive and truly release someone of an offense—without an apology—is the greatest qualifier. This is the true and measureable sign that I am in the kingdom of God. My spirit, my soul, my heart, my emotions, and sometimes my physical body will be put to the test for the sake of the kingdom. I must meet the challenge.

I invite you to practice the principle of giving beyond just an offering in the church building. That's too easy. Any one of us can give an offering. I invite you to put your grand spirituality to the test. Forgive others just as Jesus said to forgive them—over and over again. Lose count of the offenses. Be prepared to forgive. Don't demand or expect apologies. Remember your offense to your Father. Consider the kingdom and its principles. Prove your relationship with the Creator of all and give forgiveness. Nothing says you really know God like forgiveness does.

WHEN YOU FORGIVE, YOU WILL BE FORGIVEN IN HEAVEN AND ON EARTH EVEN WHEN YOU DON'T EXPECT IT.

When you do this, you can walk with the expectation that you will receive what you have given, over and over again. You will be forgiven in heaven and on earth even when you don't expect it. When you really mess up and feel like you have failed immeasurably, you will be forgiven. When you try to apologize, the offended party will quickly let you know that it is not necessary. Expect forgiveness from heaven and earth.

10

APOLOGIES HAVE FAILED US

For when we were still without strength, in due time Christ died for the ungodly. For scarcely for a righteous man will one die; yet perhaps for a good man someone would even dare to die. But God demonstrates His own love toward us, in that while we were still sinners, Christ died for us.

(Romans 5:6–8 NKJV)

While we were *still* sinners, Christ was provided for our redemption. God did not wait for an apology to offer the way of forgiveness. God made preparations for offenses by allowing the death of the Lamb of God, His son Jesus, before the foundation of the earth was laid. (See Revelation 13:8.) This divine pre-thought is inspiring. If there is a remedy for offense already in place, then the offense doesn't have the same impact.

Unfortunately, we sometimes don't look to Christ as the remedy for the offenses others commit against us; instead, we falsely substitute apologies, believing they show the authenticity of contrition and thus mark when we can extend forgiveness. I believe the enemy has put this false belief in our minds, as a counter device against the plan of God. The enemy wants us to believe the offense is more *disturbing* than the relationship is *valuable*. If the enemy can get us to believe this, then we will end our relationship with others—and perhaps even with God.

SATAN WANTS TO DELUDE US INTO BELIEVING THAT AN OFFENSE WILL OVERSHADOW OUR RELATIONSHIP WITH GOD.

I believe Satan is fully aware of God's immeasurable love—and thereby His plan to forgive—and he simply wants to delude us into believing, as he did Adam and Eve before us, that an offense will overshadow our relationship with God. Demonic influences keep us from operating as if we are guilt-free. We then perpetuate these false beliefs in our relationships. The offended wants the offender to experience some type of humiliation that matches the pain or disappointment that's been inflicted. This is viewed as justice. Yet an apology can never truly compensate in an equal way for inflicted pain. Thus, it is the adversary's trickery to make us believe that an apology is sufficient—or that it works at all.

WHAT WE EXPERIENCE WHEN WE APOLOGIZE

When we apologize, we go through a therapeutic process of remorse that includes acceptance of responsibility, acknowledgment of the hurt we caused, and some type of explanation for our role in the offense. We then indicate how we plan to be rehabilitated. In the future, we say, we will not act with such a blatant disregard for others and their feelings.

While this represents repentance—if authentic—and is a good thing, there is a problem. This cycle makes the offended seem like an errorless saint who is incapable of committing the same offense against someone else. This makes apologies therapeutic only for the offender. In effect, the *offended* never deals with being *offended* and is sure to continue to be *offended* in the future.

This is a dangerous position to be in. If this is repeated enough times, the offended becomes a self-righteous, delusional person who eventually views himself or herself merely as a victim. This can lead to someone seeing offenses when nothing offensive has happened at all. This also leads to people having no capacity to be challenged, uncomfortable, or tested.

Think for a moment about each time a person is challenged to grow. Someone with a victim mentality who is challenged to excel by a parent, teacher, boss, or mentor will view the challenge as an offense. Each time someone with a victim mentality is made to feel uncomfortable by a leader, they begin to blame the leader for the discomfort and abort the opportunity to develop as a person. Growth is stunted, maturity is delayed, opportunity for advancement backfires into regression, and the chance to gain wisdom from the experience is negated. We need a better way than mere apologies.

JESUS'S TEACHING ON ANGER AND FORGIVENESS

When it comes to how we approach our relationships, Jesus deals with the intent of the heart. In the Sermon on the Mount, Jesus said:

> *You have heard that it was said to the people long ago, 'You shall not murder, and anyone who murders will be subject to judgment.' But I tell you that anyone who is angry with a*

brother or sister will be subject to judgment. Again, anyone who says to a brother or sister, "Raca!" [a Greek term insulting one's intelligence] is answerable to the court. And anyone who says, 'You fool!' will be in danger of the fire of hell. Therefore, if you are offering your gift at the altar and there remember that your brother or sister has something against you, leave your gift there in front of the altar. First go and be reconciled to them; then come and offer your gift. Settle matters quickly with your adversary who is taking you to court. Do it while you are still together on the way, or your adversary may hand you over to the judge, and the judge may hand you over to the officer, and you may be thrown into prison. Truly I tell you, you will not get out until you have paid the last penny.

(Matthew 5:21–26)

Jesus is interpreting Old Testament Scripture in light of its intent. He is arguing against the common viewpoints of the religious leadership, beginning with the commandment against murder. (See Exodus 20:13.) Jesus doesn't deal with the criminal act alone because He knows that most people who secretly want to kill someone will never do it. He is relating the intent of murder to hatred, which is also seen in other emotions. As a result, Jesus deals with anger, demeaning others, and misidentifying the intent of other people. Jesus points out that these emotions all precede the willingness to murder. In the process, Jesus goes much deeper than the interpretations of His day, which only dealt with the criminal act of murder. Jesus deals with the heart.

Jesus tells us that we will be subject to judgment when we are angry without cause. This type of anger can exist without the other person even being aware that we're angry. And it grows as we watch someone acting or speaking in a way we oppose. This is resentment; it builds up inside you and the other person is unaware that their actions or words are bothering you.

This type of anger occurs regularly in our lives. We often believe that a spouse, friend, coworker, or child "should know better." We think, *I don't like that*—and they should just understand. We don't even give the other person the opportunity to hear from us; instead, we simply get angry. This type of anger, if left unchecked, leads to resentment.

MURDER DOESN'T JUST HAPPEN; IT STARTS WITH ANGER AND THEN GRADUATES TO DEBASEMENT.

Resentment leads to public and private insults. (See Matthew 5:22.) When we demean a person publicly or privately, calling them stupid, foolish, incompetent, and the like, we degrade their very character. Jesus teaches us how murder doesn't just happen; it starts with anger and then graduates to debasement. We eventually think so little of the person that we view them as no better than an animal and are thus willing to kill them just like we would an animal. This is how murder occurs.

Anger affects everything we do. Jesus illustrates this with an example for his first-century Jewish audience regarding Temple offerings. (See Matthew 5:23–26.) He says if you want to bring an offering to the altar—we could substitute "in worship" in modern parlance—but have an outstanding offense in your heart, it is your responsibility to first go and clear up the offense. When Jesus outlines this process, He is creating a path for dialogue and reconciliation that exceeds an apology. Jesus is suggesting a two-way street of open dialogue that the offender is initiating. Jesus is essentially saying it will be therapeutic for both parties to deal with the matter.

In the larger context, Jesus is dealing with the state of our *hearts* and not just our actions. Jesus is advocating for resolutions that will have great merit for our relationships. This is why in healthy cases of reconciliation, both parties often end up apologizing; they both realize they have contributed to the offense in some way or another.

Jesus is advocating for communication with those we have offended because it's crucial to worship—it authenticates our relationship with our God. Dealing with offenses—whether we offended someone or are the person who was offended—allows us to worship freely without distraction.

Extending forgiveness keeps me free and clear in my access to God. It avoids disruption. Imagine the kind of worship we would experience personally and publicly if we had no outstanding offenses. I believe we would really see the power of God in worship services in a whole new way.

JOSEPH'S POWERFUL EXAMPLE OF A FORGIVING SPIRIT

Learning the lessons of Christ are paramount because there are crucial relationships that we may cancel prematurely—relationships that may prove to be extremely valuable later on in life. This is the kind of thing most people don't understand when they are young, but it proves to be true when we mature. This is seen in one of the greatest stories of forgiveness in the Old Testament, the story of Joseph and his older brothers. (See Genesis 37–50.) When Joseph's brothers seek his demise early on in his life, they have no idea how valuable their relationship to Joseph will be many years later. They also cannot imagine that their brother, who they had offended so greatly, would ultimately be able to value his relationship with them more than the offense.

There is no question from reviewing the story that Joseph's older brothers intended to harm him in every way imaginable—first to kill him and then to enslave him instead. (See Genesis 37.) They didn't like Joseph's dreams and they were angry. In parallel with Jesus's teaching (see Matthew 5:21–26), their contempt was obvious by their name-calling. *"Here comes that dreamer!' they said to each other"* (Genesis 37:19). This name-calling was elevated to a plot to murder Joseph, but then the brothers decided to make some money—after throwing him into a pit—by selling him to slave traders. All of this could have rendered Joseph with no capacity to forgive, yet Joseph finds a way to move on with life, demonstrating a spirit of forgiveness. This amazing trait could be the primary reason why Joseph's life moves onward and upward regardless of the setbacks and problems he faces. Joseph shows his spirit of forgiveness each time he is wronged by others. (See Genesis 39–40.) He does not seem to carry the offense in his heart; this renders him suitable for elevation, promotion, wealth, and dominion.

JOSEPH'S INCREDIBLE ABILITY TO FORGIVE IS A TESTAMENT OF HIS EMOTIONAL BALANCE.

Joseph's incredible ability to forgive is a testament of his emotional balance. Emotional balance is a result of emotional intelligence. Joseph is my poster boy for emotional stability in that he views everything with an amazingly different perspective. This perspective was probably developed during his formative and adolescent years; he was raised and loved by a father who cared deeply for him. (See Genesis 37:3.) I believe this was the key to the emotional balance that Joseph exhibited that was absent in his brothers. Joseph understood that he was valued by his father and by God.

When we take into account all that Joseph endured—and how he responded to his brothers at the end of the story—it is clear that an apology could not have inspired Joseph to forgive. (See Genesis 42–45.) Instead, Joseph valued relationships over offenses.

When Joseph firsts encounters his brothers again, in Egypt during a famine, they have no idea who he is. Rather than revenge—which Joseph could have easily executed since the pharaoh has cloaked him in great power—his first objective is to see his youngest brother Benjamin. As events unfold and Joseph's brothers still do not know who he is, he has to hide himself so they will not see him cry. (See Genesis 42:24, 43:30.) Joseph is emotionally in touch with the situation yet somehow still forgiving. From the beginning, he looks after his brothers even though they hurt him deeply in the past.

Before his brothers can apologize, Joseph is forgiving. Ultimately, his brothers' contriteness is more therapeutic for them than it is for Joseph. He has already forgiven. Joseph's posture is powerful enough to restore an entire family, even after deep wrongs have been committed against him.

WHEN APOLOGIES WORK

Joseph's story shows that apologies work—the brothers' remorse helps to bring the family back together. But it all began with Joseph's heart.

I do believe that apologies work, just not in the way we have traditionally believed they do. The apology primarily aids the one expressing it. Unsolicited apologies allow the one who levied the offense to reflect on their actions and their repercussions. They free us to discuss our own insensitivity and possibly receive help. When both parties are able to conclude that they participated in the offense in some way, they both learn to manage future situations better.

The greatest reason that the offender should apologize is to express the *value of the relationship* to the offended and further express commitment to that relationship. When the offended already has forgiveness in place, an apology has a higher value—it helps both parties. When forgiveness is not in place, an apology will likely be viewed with skepticism.

A POSTURE OF FORGIVENESS CREATES AN OPPORTUNITY TO REINVIGORATE A RELATIONSHIP.

This is why it is so valuable to have a posture of forgiveness at the time of an offense. It allows for an apology to be more than words; it creates an opportunity to reinvigorate the relationship. It helps a relationship move into a place of humility and genuineness.

In my fifteen years of pastoring, I saw numerous people completely break down during a counseling session when they were vulnerable about their past hurts. They believed they had overcome a past pain and offered forgiveness in their hearts, but in actuality, they were guarding the emotional trauma. Having never heard an apology from the person who hurt them, they had never let go of the pain. If they had embraced a spirit of forgiveness, like Joseph did, it would have brought healing to their life. It would have also put them in a position to reconcile with the person who had previously hurt them, if the opportunity arose.

Authentic forgiveness partnered with a heartfelt apology creates an irresistible moment for a relationship to become more intimate because of the power of vulnerability. This is why authentic apologies, based on a spirit of forgiveness, are so powerful in marriages.

Apologies should involve two people being liberated and thereby feeling that something successful has taken place, that the relationship has progressed. This is especially powerful when such an outcome was originally unimaginable, such as in the case of Joseph and his brothers.

This is how we must view the forgiveness-apology equation. It must be measured by advancement in the relationship that could not have been realized without the offense scenario. In this context, the difficulty of offenses can be managed in light of a potential superior outcome. While this may not make dealing with offenses emotionally or psychologically easier, it does bring a deeper meaning and purpose into a bleak situation. As we learn how to manage and navigate offenses better, we move into a more profound and richer aspiration for each and every relationship.

Let your practice of forgiveness be habitual. Let your apologies be genuine and self-initiated. Allow purpose to arise out of every situation. Don't be overly distracted by pain and disappointment. Realize that you are capable of inflicting the same hurt on others. Don't allow the offense to become more valuable than the relationship.

11

RESTORATION, RECONCILIATION, AND REPEAT OFFENDERS

Forgiving repeat offenders tends to be the biggest challenge. Jesus said, *"Take heed to yourselves. If your brother sins against you, rebuke him; and if he repents, forgive him. And if he sins against you seven times in a day, and seven times in a day returns to you, saying, 'I repent,' you shall forgive him"* (Luke 17:3–4 NKJV). (Compare Matthew 18:21–35.)

All of my life, I have heard the phrase, "I can forgive but I can't forget" as a legitimate reason for holding on to an offense. People are truly being honest when they say they can't forget how someone has hurt them. From a psychological perspective, there is a process called rumination, whereby our brains repeatedly meditate and ponder our negative emotions and, at times, the memories affiliated with them. Jesus seems to be putting this psychological state to the test.

However, Jesus is not suggesting that we stay in harmful relationships or allow others to needlessly inflict pain. We need to understand the difference between reconciliation and restoration in the context of continual forgiveness. This will help us understand how to apply Jesus's teaching about repeat offenders.

SHOULD I REALLY JUST FORGIVE?

There is no question that some offenses can have a devastating impact on a relationship. Consider a criminal offense against society, adultery in a marriage, stealing from a company, or breaching a secret. Those who are hurt by these actions can rarely recover without serious or long-term repercussions. Even chronic tardiness or perpetual lying can cause the offended to be pushed to the edge of their ability to forgive, forget, and restore the relationship.

A question I am often asked when counseling people is, "So am I just supposed to forgive them?" When this question is posed, I know what the person is really saying is, "Do they just get away with *that* and I am supposed to return to the same level of relationship with them? How is that possible?" We've all been there to some degree or another. It leads us to wonder, "Does God expect us to just forgive and forget and return to a relationship as if everything is 'normal'?" The good news is that there is a difference between *restoration* and *reconciliation*. We must bring this into the forgiveness equation.

Although *restoration* and *reconciliation* are typically used interchangeably, they are not the same and the difference can help us discern how to manage a relationship. *Restoration* is best defined as renewal, reestablishment, or returning to some former, original, or unimpaired condition. In contrast, *reconciliation* refers to coming into harmony or agreement. While *reconciliation* often involves *restoration*, it can simply involve settling or resolving a matter.

Most of us typically view forgiveness from a *restoration* standpoint. But in the context of repeat offenders, should we apply the definition of *restoration* or *reconciliation*?

RECONCILIATION IS THE FIRST TIER WE MUST REACH IN OUR RELATIONSHIPS.

In my view, *reconciliation* is the first tier—the minimum viable tier—that we must reach in our relationships.

RECONCILIATION

To understand what *reconciliation* looks like, we must go back to the garden of Eden and examine what happens with Adam and Eve. (See Genesis 3.) After their failure to adhere to God's command, Adam and Eve experience what it means to be truly forgiven even though they never apologize. The penalty for their disobedience is placed upon an animal and they are able to walk away without dying on the spot and without reaping the wrath of YHWH. (See Genesis 3:21.) However, they were thrown out of Eden.

> And the LORD God said, "The man has now become like one of us, knowing good and evil. He must not be allowed to reach out his hand and take also from the tree of life and eat, and live forever." So the LORD God banished him from the Garden of Eden. (Genesis 3:22–2⁻

This is a clear picture of *reconciliation*. What YHW⁻ settle, resolve, and resign to something that was n⁻ Adam and Eve could continue to participate in His⁻

not as He originally intended. In other words, instead of killing them on the spot, this was the next best thing.

Reconciliation is still powerful. Knowing that Adam and Eve's egregious act was too offensive to allow them to be restored, God still allows them to go forth and replenish the earth. (See Genesis 3:23–4:1.) Reconciliation allows them to have a relationship with God, but it's now changed. What YHWH did was necessary so that Adam and Eve could have a clear understanding of what took place; their sin was not to be swept under the rug. Instead, it was acknowledged as a game-changer in their relationship with YHWH. If they were to stay in the garden and have the same access to the tree of life, it would have been catastrophic in the long run.

Sometimes, we think that changing the context of a relationship is being too harsh, ruthless, or unforgiving. But it's often the best way to preserve some level of integrity in the relationship without it becoming detrimental to all parties involved. Think for a moment of the danger of having these two people walking around the garden fully restored—having knowledge of good and evil, and seeing the tree of life every day. Wouldn't that be a worse threat to their relationship with God in the long run? Wouldn't it put a new level of strain on the relationship? Wouldn't that cause God to treat them differently from day to day? God's choice allows Him to love them from a distance, so to speak, and not utterly destroy them.

As the story progresses, there are no references to the previous level of intimacy between God and Adam, no verses about Adam hearing God's voice or divine fellowship. I'm not suggesting that YHWH didn't speak to Adam anymore or love him any less, but there is no written reference to the garden level of intimacy ever existing again. Yet Adam is able to go, *"be fruitful and multiply"* (Genesis 1:28 NKJV), and *"till the ground from which he was taken"* (Genesis 3:23 NKJV). This suggests that Adam was under the blessing of God's original intent, as well as the consequence of his failure. He enjoyed a part of his old relationship, but lived under the new context. Now if God Himself functioned in this context, then we must accept that in our own relationships, reconciliation is sometimes our best option.

Reconciliation is a necessary part of the forgiveness process for both parties. The relationship is valued over the offense, but it's operating under a new context going forward.

For example, if an employee is consistently missing the mark, the employer reevaluates their relationship. Eventually, the employee is put on probation, thus allowing a part of the relationship to be maintained while defining specifically how it can move forward. Both parties still benefit from the relationship yet remain protected from its further deterioration. The goal is to reconcile the employee-employer relationship and, ideally, restore it.

Since we are all in a growth process, this is not to be viewed as something for "them" to learn but rather something for all of us to consider. At different points in life, we will end up on different sides of the reconciliation equation—as the one offering reconciliation or the one requesting it.

RELATIONSHIPS THAT ADD NO LONG-TERM VALUE TO YOUR LIFE SHOULD BE RECONCILED TO FINALITY AS A LAST RESORT.

In this context, we don't have to deal with the dilemma of "forgive and forget" in quite the same way. Forgiveness is still in place and is always the main component. Forgetting is now renegotiated based upon the paradigm of reconciliation. We must keep in mind that both parties are imperfect and employing forgetfulness is of great value. But we must also consider the specifics of the relationship and whether remembrance is necessary. In the employee-employer example, remembrance is necessary as long as the probation is in place.

We must also consider the value of particular relationships to our life *overall*. There is a judgment call that you have to make on an individual basis. In some cases, there are relationships that add no long-term value to your life and should possibly be reconciled to finality. This still meets the requirements of the minimum definition of reconciliation—to be resigned to something not desired. Since there is no way to predict the future behavior of another—or yourself, for that matter—the decision of finality should involve deep reflection. Since we are all flawed, this is not a decision that should be made out of anger, hurt, or disappointment. Reconciliation to finality—meaning to the point of ending a relationship's presence in your life—should be a last resort. When you make this kind of decision, it should be clear to you that there is no further opportunity to reestablish the original context of the relationship.

Adam and Eve were expelled from the garden because it was impossible for them to regain the confidence of YHWH's original agreement. (See Genesis 1:15–17.) Since that agreement was breached in a way that changed the nature of Adam—he now knew good and evil—God could not take the chance that he'd also eat from the tree of life. Due to the overwhelming potential that Adam would fail Him again, God was reconciled to the fact that He had to expel him from the garden of Eden.

Regardless of how traumatic or repetitive an offense may be, the continuation of the relationship is based upon the ability to maintain the original agreement, now or in the future. The idea of an original agreement is often seen in the relationship of a mother and child. If a child is a drug abuser or a criminal, the mother is often willing to give that child another chance over and over again. She enables the relationship to continue based upon an agreement such as, "You will always be my baby," or "I can't turn my back on my child." There is an appeal to the original agreement of maternity. What that mother is really saying is that she agrees to continue in the relationship with no adjustments or requirements because she and the child agree on the maternal ties. Whenever this level of agreement is in place, the offense will always be secondary to the relationship—even if the relationship becomes unhealthy, damaging, or abusive to one party.

But this is not representative of true reconciliation. This merely shows the principle of an original agreement.

How can such a relationship shift to a context of reconciliation? Perhaps the mother has to realize that in the original, maternal agreement, the child was young, immature, and irresponsible. However, when the child is grown, the mother can no longer view her child from this perspective. Now the child must be a responsible, mature adult who takes ownership of their decisions. Once the mother accepts this reality—and makes it a condition of her agreement with the child—reconciliation can actually be applied. A healthy relationship can exist because the original agreement has been modified to reflect the new state of the child.

This is why it is so important to discern the difference between a relationship that should be reconciled and one that should be restored. The wrong application will create a distorted relationship in the long run and result in someone who never takes responsibility for their actions. This is the main reason why God reconciles with Adam and doesn't restore him to the original relationship. If God had accepted Adam's excuses as legitimate, the original agreement between them could have been restored. That would bind God to a relationship that would eventually become abusive and unhealthy. You can see a glimpse of it in Adam's answer when he blames his disobedience on *"the woman you put here with me"* (Genesis 3:12).

Adam's answer tells us that over time, there will be no growth or accountability. If God accepted this answer, then Adam would use this excuse or something similar over and over again to avoid taking ownership of his actions. Thus God would be fostering a relationship that no longer embodied His original intent. This manipulation of the relationship would cause God to function outside of His character. And it would empower Adam to continue to blame God for his failures.

No one wants to continue to feel abused or taken for granted in any relationship, whether it's with a family member, friend, neighbor, coworker, or employer. This makes reconciliation an essential part of the forgiveness equation. If the idea of reconciliation is properly incorporated into your relationships, many of them will find a more appropriate way of proceeding.

RESTORATION

Unlike reconciliation, *restoration* is not something you default to. It is something you must weigh—not in light of the *offense*, but rather based on the long-term value and purpose of the original agreement or relationship.

RESTORATION MUST BE BASED ON THE LONG-TERM VALUE AND PURPOSE OF THE ORIGINAL AGREEMENT OR RELATIONSHIP.

Let's examine this through the examples of Saul and David and their relationship with the God of Israel. Both kings made dreadful mistakes. The ultimate state of their relationship with God illustrates the difference between reconciliation and restoration.

Saul's relationship with God was *reconciled* after his offenses, but David's was *restored*. It appears that the number of offenses each committed did not play a part in their relationship with God, since David seems to have sinned as much as Saul. So why the difference?

SAUL—RECONCILIATION AND BEING BEYOND RECONCILIATION

Saul's major offense was being disobedient to the word of YHWH spoken by Samuel, the prophet and priest. We can track the movements of Saul leading up to his errors. (See 1 Samuel 10–13.) By the time we get to chapter 13, Saul has reigned over Israel for two years and has to fight the Philistines with an insufficient army. He has three thousand men while the Philistines have at least six thousand charioteers and *"soldiers as numerous as the sand on the seashore"* (1 Samuel 13:5). Saul is in big trouble. As the Israelite soldiers go into hiding or flee, Saul moves into a state of panic and fear. This causes him to move into disobedience and out of his appointed role.

Samuel had previously assured Saul that all would be well because he would join the king and his army after seven days.

> Go down ahead of me to Gilgal. I will surely come down to you to sacrifice burnt offerings and fellowship offerings, but you must wait seven days until I come to you and tell you what you are to do.   (1 Samuel 10:8)

On the seventh day, however, Saul becomes anxious and impatient. He decides to offer sacrifices—a most egregious offense since he is attempting to function in the place of the priest, which he is not anointed to do. (See 1 Samuel 13:9–14). This is an offense to YHWH because Saul is ignoring the kingdom protocol in an effort to protect his reputation. God has to deal with this or Saul will think he can function autonomously and usurp the proph-et-priest Samuel and the kingdom that ultimately belongs to YHWH.

God cannot restore Saul under such circumstances. Doing so would change the standard for the kingdom set forth by Samuel at the outset of Saul's appointment. This would reset the paradigm for all future kings. It would make them think that it is accept-able to disobey God's prophets and commands. And it would set a precedent for God to be abused and taken for granted.

On top of everything else, if God had *restored* His relationship with Saul, Samuel's role as prophet would become irrelevant, elim-inating a necessary check to the monarchy's authority. It would also interfere with the purity of the priesthood and its sacrifices.

As a result of Saul's actions, Samuel issues new parameters for the relationship going forward. Samuel tells Saul that his kingdom will be limited and will not be established eternally.

> *"You have done a foolish thing," Samuel said. "You have not kept the command the LORD your God gave you; if you had, he would have established your kingdom over Israel for all time. But now your kingdom will not endure; the LORD has sought out a man after his own heart and appointed him ruler of his people, because you have not kept the LORD's command."*
>
> (1 Samuel 13:13–14)

Saul's children did not assume the throne after him—some-one else was raised up to take his place, someone with a heart after YHWH's will and choices. God's relationship with Saul was *rec-onciled* but *not restored*. Saul is functioning under an amended ver-sion of the original agreement.

Later, Samuel again gives instructions to Saul, this time to fight the Amalekites and utterly destroy them. But again, func-tioning out of pride and fear, Saul disobeys YHWH. Instead of destroying everything, he spares the Amalekites' king, Agag, as well as their best sheep and cattle. (See 1 Samuel 15:2–9.) This offense is along the same lines as the previous one. It suggests that Saul does not properly value his reconciled relationship with God. Saul justifies his actions by telling Samuel that the soldiers *"spared the best of the sheep and cattle to sacrifice to the* LORD *your God"* (1 Samuel 15:15).

SAUL WAS OBVIOUSLY MORE CONCERNED ABOUT HIS STATUS AS KING THAN HIS RELATIONSHIP WITH GOD.

When YHWH rejects Saul this time, it is not a judgment as much as it is an acknowledgement of Saul's view of their relationship. Saul was obviously more concerned about his status as the king and his popularity than his relationship with God. YHWH does not accept Saul's claim of saving the best livestock for a sacrifice; He views this offense as a rebellion against His word. Samuel tells him:

> Does the LORD *delight in burnt offerings and sacrifices as much as in obeying the* LORD*? To obey is better than sacrifice, and to heed is better than the fat of rams. For rebellion is like the sin of divination, and arrogance like the evil of idolatry. Because you have rejected the word of the* LORD*, he has rejected you as king.*   (1 Samuel 15:22–23)

Now, God takes the kingdom away from Saul, a sign that their relationship is beyond reconciliation.

Obviously, no one can take the blameless position that God can take, but the stages and steps that God takes should be understood as a protocol for understanding when to *restore*, when to *reconcile*, and when the relationship moves *beyond reconciliation*. But before you make your final decision about a particular relationship in your life, let's look at the life of David, which offers a deeper understanding of the process.

DAVID AND RESTORATION

You might think that David's major life errors should disqualify him in the same way Saul was eventually disqualified. However, the main thing to keep in mind as we examine David's life is the value he placed on his relationship with God. This will always be the determining factor in whether a relationship should be *restored*, *reconciled*, or, in rare cases, *completely discarded*.

At the outset, it's important to recognize two things about David's character. First, YHWH recognizes the state of David's heart over his outward appearance, choosing him over his older brothers. (See 1 Samuel 16:5–10.) Second, when David runs an errand for his father, taking food to three brothers as they battle against the Philistines, he exhibits a passion for the kingdom and the name of YHWH. He hears Goliath taunting the Israelites and asks, *"Who is this uncircumcised Philistine that he should defy the armies of the living God?"* (1 Samuel 17:26). This is why David is often called "a man after God's own heart."

Scripture tells us that David had a good run until we get to 2 Samuel 11. At that point, David's flawless ascent starts on a downward spiral. He lusts after Bathsheba and impregnates her, makes sure her husband, Uriah, is sent to the battlefront, and tries to distance himself from his actions. All of these errors pose serious problems for David's relationship with God and they certainly displease Him. (See 2 Samuel 11:27.)

What happens next is very similar to what happened in the life of Saul. God sends the prophet Nathan to speak to David. (See

2 Samuel 12:1–14.) After Nathan offers a parable, he reveals that he is aware of David's sin, then delivers YHWH's verdict against David. Although it's pretty tough, it represents *restoration*, not *reconciliation*. There is no diminution in their relationship. God almost seems to be more disappointed than angry with David.

David readily admits he has sinned and Nathan tells him:

> *The LORD has taken away your sin. You are not going to die. But because by doing this you have shown utter contempt for the LORD, the son born to you [with Bathsheba] will die.*
> (2 Samuel 12:13–14)

This is clearly *restoration*. David's kingship is still intact and his authority is not diminished.

God's choice to restore His relationship with David and not merely reconcile it has nothing to do with the type of sin he committed and everything to do with the type of relationship David has with YHWH. When his failure is uncovered, David *confesses*, telling Nathan, "*I have sinned against the LORD*" (2 Samuel 12:13). No excuses, no explanations, no negotiation, or reasoning—just a true confession. Adam made an excuse, Eve had an explanation, and Saul tried to justify his actions. Others deny and some ignore, but David confessed because that was the position of his heart.

The consequences of David's actions—as declared by God through the prophet Nathan—became a reality. (See 2 Samuel 12:9–12; 17:21–22.)

Even at the most difficult times of his kingship, when others attempted to take his life or his throne, David remained the king. This speaks to the repercussions of some of his errors, but also to the restoration of his relationship with YHWH.

The story of David's life allows us to see that restoration doesn't mean that everything will be perfectly fine again. The reality is that restoration can eliminate some of the comfort and ease of the relationship; it may never return to its original state without a lot of effort and awareness. But for David, the process of failure took him to a place of maturity in his reign as king and he really doesn't fall into that trap again. When he next stumbles, there's a very different context attached to it.

David took a census of the number of men in his kingdom, going against God's wishes. (See 2 Samuel 24:1–25.) He knew immediately afterward that he had sinned and he begged God to forgive him. This is also a key difference between Saul and David. In this instance, David's response is similar to his response to his previous error. It's not an apology, but a confession. A confession is far more powerful than an apology! Each of David's confessions represents acknowledgment and ownership of his actions.

WHEN DAVID CONFESSES HIS SINS, GOD RESTORES THEIR RELATIONSHIP.

David's confidence in God is so strong that in the midst of the plague that befalls the nation because of his sin, he again cries out to God. He confesses again, but this time he is very intent on making it clear that this was *his failure* and not the failure of his people—so he should bear the burden of the God's wrath. (See 2 Samuel 24:17.) This not only confirms that he is a man after God's heart, but also that he has the heart of a true leader. This helps us see the true distinction between David and Saul—this is why Saul was *reconciled* while David was *restored*.

When David makes this second confession, the prophet Gad gives him the word of YHWH on where to erect an altar for sacrifice and peace offerings to God to remove his sin. (See 2 Samuel 24:18.) David's restoration is confirmed because he worships God just as He commands. Worship was the core of David's relationship with God—before there was a Goliath, before he killed tens of thousands of men as a leader in Saul's army, and before he was made king. After all, when he was a young boy, God protected him and his sheep from bears and lions. So David gladly offered the best sacrifice possible to reconfirm his relationship with the Almighty.

WORSHIP IS THE KEY

Worship is really the key to understanding restoration. Offenses can always serve a purpose, if we patiently endure the process. If we just jump to conclusions and allow our emotions to dominate, typically, the underlying purpose is aborted. If we decide that we will not allow the offense to be regarded over the relationship, then something much greater will be revealed. After the process, we will know how to worship more sincerely and deeply.

All of the ups and downs, twists and turns, and emotional highs and lows in David's life brought him to a place of worship, both physically and spiritually. The specific place of worship revealed by Gad is very important—it is the site of the future Temple of Jerusalem. (See 2 Samuel 24:18–25; 2 Chronicles 3:1). If David had reacted any differently, he would have ruined his opportunity to be part of one of the greatest worship transitions in Israel's history. Instead, God used David's failures to create something beautiful. David was restored in his relationship with God because there was such a deep, grand purpose for His work through him.

When you and I are faced with the reality of a true offense, we must endeavor to get past the emotional aspect as soon as possible. We must shift to the deeper purpose that is yet to be revealed. This shift will also help us discern whether a relationship should be completely *restored*, *reconciled*, or *relinquished*. We should not be quick to draw any conclusions. In every case, the process is as important as the conclusion. We must also remember that at any moment, as imperfect human beings, we can find ourselves on either side of the forgiveness equation.

RECONCILING SHOULD ALWAYS BE DONE WITH A SENSE OF LAMENT.

We should never reconcile or relinquish a relationship in anger because when the anger dissipates, we may feel differently and regret our decision. Furthermore, attempting to reconcile in anger will almost certainly yield the same results as relinquishing the relationship. Reconciling should always be done with a sense of lament. After all, we are talking about a relationship that was embarked upon with good intentions and the expectation is that it has drastically shifted. This also keeps us from carrying the baggage of a merely reconciled or relinquished relationship into the next one.

POSTSCRIPT: OUR BROKEN WORLD NEEDS FORGIVENESS

In those days there was no king in Israel; everyone did what
was right in his own eyes.
—Judges 21:25 NKJV

We live in a time like that cited in the book of Judges. Everyone does what is right in their own eyes. Families are broken. Racial tension abounds. Communities turn on one another. Churches struggle to stay unified. Our country is divided. There is animosity between nations.

All of these difficulties exist because we lack a spirit of forgiveness. We lack reconciliation at the very least—and we certainly lack restoration.

Perhaps the observance of Rosh Hashanah, celebrating God's creation, and Yom Kippur, remembering His forgiveness, can help our church communities incorporate the rhythms of forgiveness.

Let us remember what Jesus represented, that He was the Father's forgiveness incarnate. Let's be true representatives of forgiveness, forgiving as we have been forgiven, and serve as the extension of His teachings in our world.

Let's reconcile and restore, bringing together our communities by believing in the value of relationships over offenses.

And let us mend our broken world, restoring a vision of love practiced in the power and spirit of forgiveness—no apology needed.

> *Do not let any unwholesome talk come out of your mouths, but only what is helpful for building others up according to their needs, that it may benefit those who listen. And do not grieve the Holy Spirit of God, with whom you were sealed for the day of redemption. Get rid of all bitterness, rage and anger, brawling and slander, along with every form of malice. Be kind and compassionate to one another, forgiving each other, just as in Christ God forgave you.* (Ephesians 4:29–32)

ABOUT THE AUTHOR

Apostle Nathan R. Byrd is the founder and visionary leader of Jesus Makes the Difference Ministries, Inc., in New York City. He was called to the ministry at the age of nineteen under the leadership of his then pastor and older brother, Pastor Daniel H. Byrd.

Nathan served the kingdom as an evangelist for twelve years before transitioning to pastor. He then ministered at The Worship Center of St. Albans in Queens, New York, as senior pastor for fifteen years.

In 2005, Nathan was anointed and elevated to the gift of apostle, with hands laid on him by Dr. Reuben Timothy of Durban, South Africa.

Nathan is the visionary leader behind the Issachar Gathering, an annual event to discover "What now, what next?" for the body of Christ. His demanding international ministry has taken him to Thailand, Myanmar, Laos, India, Britain, Zambia, Ghana, South Africa, Kenya, Ethiopia, Ivory Coast, Tanzania, Cameroon,

Nigeria, Mexico, Canada, Colombia, Brazil, and various Caribbean islands.

In addition to *No Apology Needed: Learning to Forgive as God Does*, he authored *The Future of Worship* and *For These Reasons Shall a Man Leave His Father and Mother and Cleave to His Wife*.

Prior to entering the ministry, Nathan was employed in finance at various brokerages and banking firms on Wall Street from 1979 through 1999.

To learn more about Nathan's ministry,

visit www.jesusmakesthedifference.com

Welcome to Our House!

We Have a Special Gift for You

It is our privilege and pleasure to share in your love of Christian books. We are committed to bringing you authors and books that feed, challenge, and enrich your faith.

To show our appreciation, we invite you to sign up to receive a specially selected **Reader Appreciation Gift**, with our compliments. Just go to the Web address at the bottom of this page.

God bless you as you seek a deeper walk with Him!

WE HAVE A GIFT FOR YOU. VISIT:

whpub.me/nonfictionthx

WHITAKER
HOUSE